Black Elected Officials

Black
Elected Officials

A Study of Black Americans
Holding Governmental Office

James E. Conyers
Walter L. Wallace

Russell Sage Foundation   New York

PUBLICATIONS OF RUSSELL SAGE FOUNDATION

Russell Sage Foundation was established in 1907 by Mrs. Russell Sage
for the improvement of social and living conditions in the
United States. In carrying out its purpose the Foundation conducts
research under the direction of members of the staff or in close
collaboration with other institutions, and supports programs
designed to develop and demonstrate productive working relations
between social scientists and other professional groups. As an integral part of its operation, the Foundation from time to time pub-
lishes books or pamphlets resulting from these activities. Publication
under the imprint of the Foundation does not necessarily imply
agreement by the Foundation, its Trustees, or its staff with the
interpretations or conclusions of the authors.

Russell Sage Foundation
230 Park Avenue, New York, N.Y. 10017

© 1976 by Russell Sage Foundation. All rights reserved.
Library of Congress Catalog Card Number: 74-30881
Standard Book Number: 87154-206-4
Printed in the United States of America

To the memory of

W. E. B. DuBois

author of *The Philadelphia Negro,*
one of the earliest empirical studies in American sociology,
and of *Black Reconstruction,*
a study of the first Black elected officials.

Contents

Preface

As far as we know, data of the kind discussed here have not been available until now. We are aware, however, that the effort to get them into public view before they take on purely historical interest has cost our discussion something in reduced analytic rigor. Our discussion is offered, therefore, as a stimulus to more definitive research by our social science colleagues and in the belief that it will be of topical interest to the Black elected officials who are its subjects, to the Black community, and to the public at-large.

The terms "Black" and "White" are capitalized here because we regard them as proper nouns when referring to the race-ethnicity of persons. We therefore treat them as we do all other terms having this general type of reference—terms such as "Anglo-Saxon," "Chicano," "Jamaican," "Protestant," "Negroid," "Caucasoid," and so on.

James E. Conyers
Walter L. Wallace

Acknowledgments

This collaboration is a product of a friendship that began nearly twenty years ago, when we were both students of sociology at Atlanta University. We offer it in remembrance of those good times and of our fellow students, and especially in appreciation of our teachers there, Mozell C. Hill and Hylan G. Lewis.

We each played some part in almost every phase of this research, but in the division of primary responsibilities Conyers was study director. He conceived the research and supervised the collection, coding, processing, and transcription of its data. Wallace performed the data analysis and wrote this report of findings and speculations.

Russell Sage Foundation supported the entire study financially and in many other ways. We especially appreciate the help of Orville G. Brim, Jr., whose Foundation presidency witnessed the beginning of this study, and Hugh F. Cline, whose presidency witnesses its completion.

Indiana State University has our appreciation for handling financial transactions, making available computer resources, and printing questionnaires. The following students at that university gave valuable research and clerical assistance: Ronald Luedeman, David Prestipino, Barbara Stocker, Shirley Norris, Christine Chatman, Cheryl Coles, and Gwendolyn Locke.

We also thank the following persons and their organizations for help at crucial points during the study: Frank D. Reeves, former director, Joint Center for Political Studies, Washington, D.C.; John Lewis, director, Voter Education Project, Atlanta, Georgia; Eleanor Farrar, director, Washington Office, Metropolitan Applied Research Center; the Honorable Robert B. Blackwell, mayor, Highland Park, Michigan, former chairman of the National Black Caucus of Local Elected Officials; State Senator Mervyn M. Dymally of California; and Ernest E. Juillerat, assistant executive director, National School Boards Association.

Professors Mack Jones of Atlanta University, Edgar Epps, University of Chicago, Edsel Erickson, Western Michigan University, and Martin Levin, Emory University, were consultants to the study in its early stages, and we value the advice they gave. We also gratefully acknowledge the help given by Professors Charles V. Hamilton, Columbia University, Tobe Johnson, Morehouse College, and most especially, Herbert McClosky, the University of California at Berkeley, and Hylan G. Lewis of the Metropolitan Applied Research Council and Brooklyn College, who read and criticized the manuscript in highly constructive ways.

A special note of appreciation is reserved for Patricia Murphy Kruidenier, Steve McCloud, and Joan Pifer—each of whom provided essential help during different phases of this research. Pat Kruidenier kept records and other information sources, requisitioned materials, drew samples, transcribed interviews, mailed questionnaires, and was literally indispensable to the data collection phase. Steve McCloud skillfully shepherded the questionnaire data through the computer. Joan Pifer of Russell Sage Foundation provided an extraordinarily high degree of expertise and patience in typing the manuscript, to which Dorothy Brothers and Gerry McQueen of the Center for Advanced Study in the Behavioral Sciences put the finishing touches.

While gratefully acknowledging all of the above help, the authors take sole responsibility for the design, execution, analysis, conclusions, and speculations of this study.

J. E. C.
W. L. W.

Black Elected Officials

CHAPTER 1 □□

Blacks Elected to Government: A "Second Reconstruction"?

Several scholars have proposed that since World War II the United States has experienced a "Second Reconstruction" with reference to the direction and amount of government intervention in Black-White relations (see Wilson, 1965; Woodward, 1966; Feagin and Hahn, 1970; and Kilson, 1971). Although this analogy carries positive implications with respect to the accomplishments of Reconstruction, the speed with which these accomplishments were swept away is an ill omen indeed.

> Twenty-one Negroes served in the House of Representatives, from the 43rd through the 56th Congress, 1865-95. . . . Negroes were also elected to the state legislatures during the Reconstruction period. . . .

> By 1902, there was not a single Negro in a state legislature and not a single Negro in the national Congress. In addition, the Southern states adopted numerous devices to prevent Negroes from voting: intimidation, laws setting up property and poll tax requirements, the famous "grandfather clause" . . . and the "lily-white" primary. These political measures were followed by the resegregation of those institutions which had been desegregated during Reconstruction, including state universities and other public facilities (Fleming, 1966:420,423).

Thus, the "Second Reconstruction" analogy clearly requires us to examine the likelihood of a second "redemption" and "reunion"—a second White supremacist restoration. How likely is it that the Black community's political gains since World War II will become more deeply and

1

broadly extended rather than overthrown? The importance of Blacks elected to government in the United States must finally be assessed in light of this question.

Let us briefly consider one historian's explanation of how the final vestiges of Reconstruction were erased at the end of the last century, and how a "Second Reconstruction" began during the middle of this century. C. Vann Woodward (1966) argues that the South's adoption of extreme racism was the result of two events: American imperialism in the Pacific and Caribbean, which generated pressures toward national unity between northern and southern Whites, and the agrarian economic depression, which generated pressures toward class division among southern Whites. These two events, says Woodward, combined to produce a general, nationwide relaxation of White opposition to racism. In the North, "as America shouldered the White man's burden, she took at the same time many Southern attitudes on the subject of race," and in the South "the Negro was . . . pressed into service as a sectional scapegoat in the reconciliation of estranged White classes."

What followed was a wave of intense racism throughout the country that continued, essentially without abatement, into World War II. Then, says Woodward, some time during the war, the tide turned again and the United States entered a "Second Reconstruction." Woodward offers the following explanation for this change: "Amoral and impersonal forces" (including especially Black migration out of the South and out of rural areas, and international conflicts with fascism and communism) finally moved "practical politicians and strategists of the two great political parties to take an interest" in the anti-racist ideas long advocated by the NAACP, the Harlem Renaissance writers and artists, the social gospel movement in the White churches, and southern White liberals. Having thus come to *want* to take anti-racist steps, Woodward claims, politicians were *enabled* to do so by concentration of governmental power at the federal level (resulting from the great Depression of the 1930s, world war, and postwar international conflict), and were forcibly *pressed* to do so by the Black community and its allies through the sit-in movement, the voter registration movement, and the several urban uprisings of the 1960s.

During this period, southern Black voter registration rose from 5 percent of its potential in 1940 to 20 percent in 1952, and then to 38 percent in 1964 (Campbell and Feagin, 1974). And in the 1964 election, 280 Blacks were elected to public office throughout the nation, including 6 congressmen, 90 state legislators, and 184 other state and local officers (Pinkney, 1969:106). By 1971, southern Black voter registration stood at 59 percent of its potential (Campbell and Feagin, 1974) and 1,860 Blacks held elective government office throughout the country (Joint Center for Political Studies, 1971). In 1974, the voter registration figure was probably still around 59 percent and 2,991 Blacks held elective office (Joint Center for Political Studies, 1974).

Now, regarding the question of whether these trends are likely to continue or be reversed, we believe that one must take into account several differences between the present social context of Black-White relations in the United States and the context in which the overthrow of Reconstruction occurred some 80 years ago.

The first pair of differences refers to the spatial distribution of the Black population, i.e., its regional dispersion and its urban concentration. The fact that the Black population has lost much of its concentration within the southern region means that the political gains of the Black community are not regionally confined, nor are they likely to be regionally eradicated, as was Reconstruction. Reconstruction was overthrown by northern Whites simply releasing the South as an entire region and allowing southern Whites to handle "their" Blacks as they saw fit. But any overthrow of post-World War II gains seems to require consensus among Whites at least state-by-state, and often metropolitan area-by-metropolitan area as well. Such many-leveled and multiple consensuses would be more difficult to achieve than was the relatively simple North-South regional consensus of 1877 and the turn of the century.

Urban concentration means that the post-World War II gains were not those of a Black population largely composed of isolated farm families and small town communities. The many massively shared experiences of rural-to-urban migration, physically dense and precarious center-city living, the attainment of substantially universal literacy, the development of an urban middle class, and the repeated emergence of urban-based mass movements have made Black Americans increasingly self-conscious, politically sophisticated, and articulate. Add to this the fact that Black urban concentration has been accompanied by White suburbanization. As a result of both these population migrations, the center-city populations in all regions of the country have grown increasingly Black and thus increasingly capable of electing Blacks to high municipal office, and of contributing importantly to the election of Blacks at county, state, and federal levels of government.

The second set of differences between the social contexts of Black-White relations now and at the turn of the century refers to changes in occupation and education. When the White labor force shifted from farming, it moved heavily into white collar work, but when the Black labor force made the same shift, it was shunted almost entirely into manual and service work (see Ginzberg and Hiestand, 1966:221). And although Black workers have been entering white collar occupations in much larger num-

bers since the early years of World War II than ever before, this occupation (and income) inequality still persists. In particular, the proportion of
the White labor force that consists of proprietors, managers, and officials
increased from about 7 percent in 1910 to about 9 percent in 1960; for the
Black workers, however, the figure has remained in the neighborhood of
1 percent, except for one census date, 1950, in which it rose to 2 percent
(Ginzberg and Hiestand, 1966:220).[1] As a direct consequence of continued
economic subordination of Blacks and of the Black community, the emi-
gration of White population from the center cities has meant a net loss of
urban financial power. Therefore, to a tragically ironic extent, "Black politicians are coming to power at a time when the central city is falling apart"
(Walton, 972:201).

Changes in educational attainment have, of course, accompanied
these occupational shifts among Blacks and Whites, and persistent racial
inequalities in the latter area have their parallels in the former. Thus, the
illiteracy rate of non-Whites was about seven times that of Whites in 1900
and was still about five times that of Whites in 1969 (U.S. Census, 1960:
214, and 1973:116). But the absolute drop over those years in illiteracy
among non-Whites from 44.5 percent to 3.6 percent[2] (U.S. Census, 1960:
214 and 1973:116) may be a far more significant difference than the persistent relative difference, because it means that a larger percentage of the
Black population can become cosmopolitan with respect to the worldwide
information and ideology currents to which literacy gives access. In part,
the "revolution in expectations" among American Blacks is very likely a
consequence of our greater participation in the increasingly literate communication among all cultures.

The third set of differences reflects the changing relationship of the
United States to other nations. In the process of becoming a superpower,
the United States waged war against the racist Nazi regime and was therefore pressed into much more anti-racist official positions at home and
abroad than it might have taken otherwise. These official positions have
been repeatedly affirmed and elaborated since then, under the pressure of
national competition with avowedly anti-racist communist regimes for
the allegiance of non-White peoples the world over. Indeed, the competition with communist regimes has been so intense that even the Korean

---

[1] The U.S. Census (1973:234) shows that in 1971, the year of our survey, 12 percent of White workers and 4 percent of "Negro and Other" workers were in this
category. The inclusion of other non-Whites in the latter figure very probably raises it
from what it would be for Blacks alone.

[2] These figures are not precisely comparable, however, since the first is a percentage of all non-Whites age 10 years and older, while the second is a percentage of those
age 14 years and older.

and Vietnam wars—which carried strong racist overtones—were not per-mitted to reverse these official positions.

Fourthly, the attitudes of Blacks and Whites toward themselves and toward each other very probably are different now from what they were at the end of the nineteenth century. More Black Americans take pride in themselves than before, and fewer accept belief in their racial inferiority. Blacks have had much more experience with the politics of resistance in many areas of American life than 75 years ago, and each new movement toward freedom seems more massive and race-wide than the previous one. White Americans probably also respect Blacks more, and probably fewer of them believe that Blacks are genetically inferior.

Of course, there are no survey data that can be brought to bear on these assertions regarding attitude differences between 1900 and 1975. But from a comparison of survey data collected from samples of Blacks and Whites in the population of the United States in 1964, 1968, and 1970 —bracketing the years of maximum Black urban rebellion and of White electoral reaction—Campbell concludes:

> It cannot be doubted that since World War II there has been a massive shift in the racial attitudes of white Americans. This is demonstrated not only by the evidence of opinion polls taken during this period but also by the various acts of Congress, state legislatures, and municipalities intended to protect the civil rights of black people. This is not to say that the white population have come to a full commitment to racial equality and racial justice; the data from our surveys demonstrate how far they are from that position. But there has been a current in white attitudes, away from the traditional belief in white superiority and the associated patterns of segregation and discrimination and toward a more equalitarian view of the races and their appropriate relations (1971:159).

All of this suggests that any new racist reaction may have to contend with greater subjective resistance on the part of both racial groups.

Finally, two changes should be mentioned that do not seem in them-selves to work either against or for a racist resurgence; instead, they seem to exert a catalytic effect on Black-White relations, regardless of the direc-tion that these relations take. We refer to (1) the increasing sophistication of physical technologies whereby goods, services, information, and beliefs are created and delivered and (2) the increasing influence of government —especially at the federal level—relative to other institutional sectors of American life. Both of these factors seem to imply that changes occurring in Black-White relations, whatever the direction of these changes, are apt to occur with greater speed and uniformity across the entire country. Since the present balance seems tipped against extreme racism, sophisticated technology and strong government now tend to add their weights in that direction.

We believe that all of these developments since Reconstruction jointly gave rise to the new political status of the Black community. Clearly, the Black elected officials who are the subjects of this study represent a major component of that status. But more than that, Black elected officials also constitute an essential resource for its consolidation and extension. Just as the Voting Rights Act of 1965 facilitated its own renewal in 1970 by encouraging the registration of Black voters, so the presence of Blacks in elected government positions, for the first time in significant numbers since the beginning of the century (and, indeed, in greater numbers than ever before), is not only a manifestation of the Black community's political advance but a principal guarantee that that advance will continue.

Of course, the proportion that Blacks represent of all elected government officials is still extremely small, and from this point of view their presence in government is still only "token." But it is one thing to be a token Black in, say, a university or business firm (however important that may be), and quite another to be a token Black elected to government. Regardless of Watergate, governmental organizations still retain the unquestioned power to make and enforce decisions of great import for public affairs, and as a result, governmental office still carries high prestige in the public eye. By competently holding such office, Blacks in government demonstrate to other Blacks the practicality of self-respect and the feasibility of high aspirations and to Whites the inefficiency and injustice of racial discrimination and, most importantly, the certainty of powerful and sophisticated Black opposition to such discrimination.

But still more important than the concomitants of prestige are the concomitants of power, and a share in the exercise of governmental power is highly consequential for any minority. Indeed, given the rules by which governmental organizations (especially legislative ones) operate in the United States, it is possible for even a single representative to affect the exercise of governmental power in crucial ways that may sometimes amount to a veto. Of course, it is not likely that a *single* representative will struggle for long against a large and insistent majority—although such individuals are not unknown in history. The presence of even one ally greatly strengthens an individual's independence from majority pressure, and the more numerous the minority, the more independent it can become. Thus, the fact that Black elected officials now number almost 3,000 carries great significance, despite the minute proportion of the total that figure represents. In addition, it should be pointed out that these officials are often in direct and continuing contact with one another and can thus support each other.

We expect that developments sustaining the present political gains of the Black community will continue, albeit at changing levels of intensity, for some years to come. But catastrophe can alter any continuity, and economic depression is one imaginable catastrophe.

By and large, when a pervasive economic change—whether the onset of prosperity or of depression—has occurred, most Blacks and Whites have experienced the same direction (but different degrees) of absolute change in their levels of living. Such absolute change, whether up or down, generally seems to be experienced as a "loosening" in the system, and each group seems stimulated by that experience to compare its own change with the other group's in order to make sure the loosening does not result in a loss of relative status. It is in this mutual comparison of change, rather than of condition, that notions of what constitutes racial justice and injustice seem to be most attentively spelled out and negotiated. Being the last hired in prosperity and being the first fired in depression have been equally unjust, because each has meant relative status loss for Blacks and gain for Whites, regardless of whether the absolute change has been up or down.

In the event of a new economic depression (or any sharp economic change) some White Americans will surely intensify efforts to impose a relative status loss on Black Americans. And for their part, Black Americans will try harder to move closer to equality with Whites through a relative status gain. Depending on the depth, duration, and quality of economic depression, these two tendencies will come into more or less sharp and widespread conflict. The durability of whatever gains the nation makes toward a genuine democracy would be most severely threatened in such an emergency. But government now exerts much greater control over employment practices and other determinants of level of living than it has in the past. For this compelling reason, Blacks in government constitute a new and powerful defense of the Black community against such "extraordinary" threats, as they will against more "normal" ones.

Black elected officials in government, for all of the preceding reasons, certainly deserve to be studied. We believe they are crucial to the future of the Black community and of the nation as well. However, to our knowledge, this is the first such nationwide survey. We hope that this study will reveal some new information about this group of Black Americans, and we also hope that it will have practical value in providing some factual grounds for inventing new ways whereby the size of the group may be increased. And clearly, the number of Blacks in government must be drastically increased in the years to come, if government is even to approach racial representativeness. In 1971, when our data were collected,

1,860 Black Americans held elective office at all levels of government. This number stands in dramatic contrast with the beginning of the century and is almost seven times the number reported in 1964. Now, as we complete this report some three years later, 2,991 Black Americans hold elective office in the United States, representing an increase of 61 percent over the 1971 figure. *But against these facts it should be remembered that there are about 520,000 elected government officials in the United States* (Joint Center for Political Studies, 1974:xxv), *and therefore even the present record number of Blacks among them constitutes just six-tenths of 1 percent of the total.*

We refer the reader to Tables 1.1 and 1.2 for some general information regarding the distribution of Black elected officials. In Table 1.1, for example, an examination of regional differences in the total number of Black elected officials indicates that about 50 percent of such persons hold office in the 16 southern states and District of Columbia (the exact percentage has increased from 48 percent in 1970 and 1971 to 54 percent in 1974). Further, it can be seen that consistently larger percentages of Black officials have held city and county offices in the South than in the North, but the reverse has been true of state and education offices.

Table 1.2 presents a breakdown of types of offices in the 1971 and in the 1974 *Roster* data. Our attempt here is to compare the South-North distributions of Black officials within each type of office and to show the extent to which these distributions may have changed between 1971 (the year of our data-collection) and 1974. The only large regional differences to be found at either date are in the "Law" type of office. Here we find that a much smaller percentage of Black law officials in the South than in the North are judges and magistrates, but larger percentages of such officials in the South than in the North are constables and marshals, justices of the peace, and other. Moreover, the 1974 data show that these differences have widened since 1971. This persistent South-North difference in the offices held by Black elected law officials is reflected in our samples (see Table 1.3) and in certain regional differences in law officials' personal backgrounds and other features that will be discussed in later chapters.

The Present Study

Now, having briefly sketched our view of the broader context in which this book may be placed, we turn to the study itself. Our basic data come from a nationwide survey (using a mailed questionnaire[3]) of 799 Black men and women holding office at state, county, and city levels of

---

[3] See Appendix A.

Table 1.1. Types of Office Held by All Black Elected Officials, by Region and Date (Percent)[a]

Type of Office[d]	South[b]					North[c]				
	1970	1971	1972	1973	1974	1970	1971	1972	1973	1974
Federal	—	*	*	*	*	1	1	1	1	1
State	8	8	7	6	6	15	14	11	12	11
County	7	8	10	11	11	6	6	5	5	4
City	51	48	49	45	51	34	37	34	35	39
Law	16	17	12	14	11	13	13	11	12	12
Education	18	19	20	23	21	30	30	38	36	33
Total	100 (702)e	100 (882)	100 (1074)	100 (1381)	100 (1609)	100 (767)	100 (978)	100 (1190)	100 (1240)	100 (1382)

[a] Computed from data in *National Roster of Black Elected Officials*, Washington, D.C.: Metropolitan Applied Research Center and Voter Education Projects, February 1970; and in *National Roster of Black Elected Officials*, Washington, D.C.: Joint Center for Political Studies, Vols. 1–4, March 1971, March 1972, May 1973, and April 1974.

[b] South = South Atlantic (Md., Del., W. Va., N.C., S.C., Ga., Fla., Va., D.C.); East South Central (Ky., Tenn., Ala., Miss.); West South Central (Okla., Ark., Tex., La.).

[c] North = Middle Atlantic (N.Y., N.J., Pa.); New England (Conn., Mass., N.H., Vt., R.I., Me.); East North Central (Wisc., Ill., Ind., Mich., Ohio); West North Central (Minn., Iowa, Mo., Kans., Neb., S. Dak., N. Dak.); Mountain West (N. Mex., Ariz., Nev., Utah, Colo., Wyo., Idaho, Mont.); Pacific West (Cal., Ore., Wash.), Non-continental U.S.A. (Alaska, Hawaii).

[d] Federal = U.S. senator or representative; State = senator, representative or other state office; County = County commissioner or other county office; City = city mayor or vice-mayor, councilman or alderman, or other city office; Law = judge or magistrate, constable or marshal, justice of the peace, or other law enforcement office; Education = school board member or other education office.

[e] In all tables here, parentheses enclose the number of cases on which the associated percentage is based.

* Less than 1 percent.

Table 1.2. Offices Held by All Black Elected Officials, by Type of Office and
Region, 1971 and 1974 (Percent)[a]

| | 1971 | | 1974 | |
	South	North	South	North
Senator	—	8	—	8
Representative	100	92	100	92
Federal total	100 (2)	100 (12)	100 (4)	100 (13)
Senator	19	17	14	18
Representative	81	80	86	80
Other[b]	—	3	—	2
State total	100 (70)	100 (132)	100 (90)	100 (149)
Commissioner, Supervisor[c]	82	89	82	85
Other	18	11	18	15
County total	100 (66)	100 (54)	100 (181)	100 (61)
Mayor, Vice-Mayor[d]	11	9	13	12
Councilman, Alderman	85	81	81	77
Other	4	9	6	12
City total	100 (433)	100 (352)	100 (820)	100 (540)
Judge, Magistrate	26	85	18	87
Constable, Marshal[e]	29	12	52	10
Justice of the Peace	38	2	25	2
Other	7	1	4	1
Law total	100 (143)	100 (131)	100 (179)	100 (161)
College Board	—	3	1	5
Local School Board	99	97	99	95
Other	1	—	1	—
Education total	100 (168)	100 (297)	100 (335)	100 (458)

[a] Computed from data in *National Roster of Black Elected Officials*, Washington,
D.C.: Joint Center for Political Studies, Vols. 1 and 4, March 1971 and April 1974.

[b] 1974 data include state executive.

[c] 1971 data include election commissioner.

[d] 1974 data include mayor pro-tem.

[e] 1974 data include chief of police, sheriff.

government, in courts and law enforcement agencies, and on school
boards and other public educational agencies. In addition, we conducted
personal interviews[4] with 34 Black officials, including 6 United States
representatives.

---

[4] See Appendix B.

Our study is organized around eight principal questions.

1. What *political beliefs* do Black elected officials hold?
2. What are their *motivations for seeking office?*
3. What are their *personal background characteristics?*
4. What are the characteristics of the *election districts* they represent?
5. What are their *party affiliations* and *types of elective office?*
6. What *sources of election help* did they draw upon?
7. What *impacts* have they had?
8. What *expectations* do they have?

In addition to presenting answers to each of these questions separately, we also examine some of their interconnections—indeed, such interconnections are the main content of this book. For example, we investigate how Black officials' political beliefs are related to their motivations for seeking office. And we investigate how each of those attitudinal characteristics related to Black officials' personal characteristics, and so on.

Plan of Analysis

After some closing words in this chapter regarding certain limitations imposed by our methods, we proceed to the analysis itself. Chapter 2 describes Black officials' political beliefs and motivations for seeking elective office. In Chapter 3, we describe personal background, election district, and political-governmental characteristics and then show how officials' beliefs and motivations are related to them. Chapter 4 assesses the bearing of officials' sex on all of the characteristics set forth in Chapters 2 and 3, including especially three political beliefs that relate directly to sex roles. In Chapter 5, we examine the extent to which our respondents perceived their elections had been helped or hindered by help from the Black community, the White community, political party apparatuses, and the mass media. We also assess the impact of all the factors set forth in preceding chapters on officials' perceived success in getting election help from the listed sources. Chapter 6 is devoted almost entirely to interview quotations from Black officials regarding their impact on the Black community and on the White community and regarding the future of Black-White relations in the United States. Finally, in Chapter 7, we try to draw some general conclusions from our analysis.

Methodological Cautions

Before we examine any of our data, five methodological considerations must be mentioned because they lead to strong cautions regarding interpretations of these data. The first consideration refers to our samples. When we began collecting questionnaire data for this study, the most complete known roster of Black elected officials (obtained from the Joint Center for Political Studies, Washington, D.C.) showed 1,860 such persons, including 14 United States representatives and 1 senator. On April 28, 1971, we mailed questionnaires to each of them, and after several follow-ups we received the last questionnaire from a Black elected official on January 28, 1972 (90 percent of returns were received by August 12, 1971). At that time a total of 805 usable questionnaires had been received from Black elected officials, including 6 from federal officials (which we removed from our survey analysis because they were too few to be subjected to separate statistical examination and because they were so few as to invite personal identification by our readers). As a result, the quantitative data of this report are based on an approximately 43 percent return from the 1,846 known Black elected officials at all levels of government except federal.[5]

The focus of this study is on Black elected officials. But in the survey analysis we compare these officials with a sample of White elected officials drawn to match the population of Black elected officials on type of office and geographical location. It is important to emphasize that our sample of White officials was drawn solely for its comparability to the population of Black elected officials and not for its representativeness of the population of White elected officials. The only function of our White officials sample is to estimate the difference that an official's race makes, when his or her type of office and region of the country are held constant. Therefore, no conclusions whatever should be drawn from this sample regarding White elected officials in general.

The White sample was drawn using a variety of sources, including lists, rosters, directories, almanacs, manuals, and other information supplied by state secretaries of state, the National School Boards Association, state superintendents of public instruction, the National League of Cities, the National Association of Counties, the Council of State Governments, the Office of Law Enforcement Administrative Assistance, the North American Judges Association, the National College of State Trial Judges, the National Council of Juvenile Court Judges, the National Institute of Municipal Law Offices, and the *Municipal Yearbook*, published by the International City Management Association. We matched person for per-

---

[5] Fifty-eight names on the original Roster were found to be persons no longer in office, appointed, non-Black, or deceased at the time of our data collection. If these were the only such persons on the original roster, the eligible universe would be reduced to 1,788 and our sample would be raised to about 45 percent of that total.

son. That is, in each case, we selected a White official (i.e., an official whose name was not on our list of Black officials) to match a given Black official as nearly as possible on specific locality and specific office held. Where more than one White official in a given locality seemed to match a given Black official (e.g., in the case of a Black school board member), the selection was made randomly. Where no White official in the same locality could match the office held by a given Black official exactly (as in the case of a Black mayor, for example), we selected a White official of the same office but in a closely neighboring locality.

We were faced with several difficulties in drawing and collecting data from the White sample, including the lack of up-to-date or complete lists from several states and pressure to complete our data collection from both samples during roughly the same time period and as much before the general elections of 1972 as possible. As a result, we mailed questionnaires[6] to only 1,252 (rather than the desired 1,860) White elected officials on October 29, 1971. Between that date and February 17, 1972, when the last usable questionnaire was received from a White elected official, we collected a total of 486 questionnaires (90 percent of these were received by December 29, 1971), including 2 from officials at the federal level that are not included in our analysis. We therefore have available for analysis about 39 percent of the 1,252 White elected officials to whom we sent questionnaires, and this constitutes a White sample of about 61 percent of the sample of Black elected officials.[7]

Since we tried to get completed questionnaires from 100 percent of the 1,860 elected officials, our 43 percent return prohibits drawing any definitive conclusions about that universe from this study. But it should be emphasized that the composition of our Black sample, with respect to current office held and region of the country, is not very different from that of the universe from which it was drawn. Table 1.3 presents the relevant data, and from them it may be calculated that 44 percent of our Black sample is southern (see Table 1.1 for the states included here)—a figure not widely divergent from the 48 percent of the universe of Black elected officials that was southern at the time of our data collection. In this comparison, as well as in the more detailed comparisons of current office held that this table provides, our Black sample seems representative enough to permit the exploratory analysis to which we have subjected it

[6] See Appendix A.

[7] We have a total of 1,283 usable questionnaires for our survey analysis (i.e., 799 from Black officials and 484 from White officials). However, the number of cases presented in most of our tables will be less than this, and the number will also vary from table to table, because we omitted any respondent who did not supply information on all of the variables shown in a given table.

and to make our results useful as guides for future research. In addition, Table 1.3 indicates that our White sample is not sharply divergent, with respect to the variables on which we sought comparability, from our Black sample and therefore it too seems qualitatively adequate to the uses we will make of it in this analysis.

Finally, regarding our interview sampling procedures, the officials were selected not only to reflect variation in region, rural-urban locality, and type of office, but also on the basis of our impression of their political and governmental prestige, power, and experience (as well as, of course, their availability to be interviewed). Three things need to be emphasized here: The criteria for selecting these interviewees were highly impressionistic; these criteria explicitly ruled out representativeness of Black elected officials in general; and officials at the federal level are included here, whereas none are included in the questionnaire survey analysis.

Table 1.3. Current Office Held by All Black Elected Officials in 1971[a], by Black Elected Officials in Our Sample and by White Elected Officials in Our Sample (Percent)

Current Office	Universe	South Black Sample	White Sample	Universe	North Black Sample	White Sample
State						
Senator, Representative	8	10	16	13	12	18
Other	* [b]	—	*	*	*	*
County						
Commissioner, Supervisor	6	7	6	5	6	1
Other	1	3	*	1	3	2
City						
Mayor, Vice-Mayor	5	9	13	3	5	9
Councilman, Alderman	42	40	32	29	26	19
Other	2	3	*	3	5	2
Law						
Judge, Magistrate	4	4	4	11	13	8
Constable, Marshal	5	3	3	2	*	*
Justice of the Peace and Other	7	4	6	*	1	1
Education						
School Board Member	19	18	20	30	28	38
College Board Member and Other	*	—	*	1	1	1
Totals	100 (880)	100 (338)	100 (220)	100 (966)	100 (434)	100 (258)

[a] Computed from *National Roster of Black Elected Officials*, Washington, D.C.: Joint Center for Political Studies, Vol. 1, March 1971.

[b] Less than 1 percent.

Our second methodological caution springs from the fact that this is a questionnaire and interview study exclusively. Our data are therefore based entirely on the expressed memories, beliefs, and opinions of our respondents. Since we have not made attempts to verify any of these expressions, we must allow for the possibility that, for example, the constituencies that our officials *told* us did the most in getting them elected may not have been the ones that *actually* did the most to get them elected. In noting this, we acknowledge, first, the frequent inability of a self-administered written questionnaire or a brief personal interview to convey precisely the questions that the investigator intends to ask, and second, the fallibility of even the best intentioned and most precisely understanding respondents in recording their perceptions, judgments, and memories.

On the other hand, certain considerations favor a study of this kind. For one thing, even if the actual facts were different from the way our respondents perceived them, still, real beliefs—even about unreal things —have real consequences and often these are more important than the consequences of less subjective facts. Thus, officials' *beliefs* about their election help may be more important for, say, their distribution of patronage than the actual fact of the matter. Moreover, some facts are known only to the respondents, and there can be no wholly external or independent verification of them. Foremost among such facts, of course, are the respondents' attitudes—opinions, ideologies, motivations, assessments, and projections—variables that will play prominent roles in our analysis.

Our third caution emphasizes that with only two exceptions (party affiliation and type of office), all questionnaire variables have been dichotomized. Such dichotomization has drawbacks: It prevents discovery of curvilinear relationships, and reduces the sensitivity of measures of linear relationships, which is here reduced further by our choice of Yule's Q (gamma), a relatively insensitive, but easily calculated, measure of association (Goodman and Kruskal, 1954). Still, we chose to dichotomize because we want to facilitate cross-tabulations of the highest possible order, given our case base. In other words, we want to be able to make statements not only about the sampled Black elected officials in general, but more specifically, for example, about those Black elected officials in southern states who are ideologically liberal (or conservative), and who also had constituencies containing relatively few (or many) Blacks. Dichotomizing variables near or at their medians makes it possible to do this, because, in a study based on cross-tabulations, it best "extends" our case base.

Fourthly, the reader should note that we have employed no statistical tests of significance. Given the limitations of our samples, such tests seemed more apt to mislead than enlighten the reader by endowing certain findings with an unverifiable generality. Therefore, instead of a series of rigorous tests of hypotheses, we offer our analysis as exploratory, where even the strongest relationships may not be considered definitive of the entire population of Black elected officials, but where even weak relationships may suggest hypotheses for further examination.

Finally, although causal interpretations are expressed in much of the analysis here, our claims in this regard are not strong, scientifically speaking, for the following reasons. At least three requirements seem generally accepted as justifying the causal interpretation of data: The effect must be shown to be absent or diminished when the cause is absent or diminished; the cause must be shown to precede the effect in time; and a competent audience must be persuaded that the precise spatiotemporal path through which influence was transmitted from cause to effect could, in principle, be satisfactorily[8] traced.

Regarding the first requirement, we are on fairly firm ground in this study because there is sizable variability on all items whose correlations are examined here, and on its face, admittedly without systematic validity and reliability checks, that variability seems "real" and reliable to us. Regarding the second requirement, however, our data offer only weak approximations since all variables were measured at approximately the same time—i.e., the time that respondents were actually filling out the questionnaires or being interviewed. As a result, we cannot know with certainty, for example, whether an official's self-reported attitudes, or even some personal background or election district characteristics, actually antedated the election help he or she reported receiving; the reverse sequence remains possible. For the third requirement (i.e., specification of intervening steps in the transmission of influence from presumed cause to presumed effect) we have at our disposal only a very few variables, a limited case base, and crude techniques. We simply assume that if evidence or argument can be provided here regarding a few intervening steps in a possible transmission process, "common understanding" will fill in, without calling for evidence on the rest of the process.

Now against this background of reasons for this study, its overall structure, and some methodological caveats, let us turn to our data and to the questions they help answer.

---

[8] This, of course, is a key term, because the criteria of "satisfaction" vary from discipline to discipline, from culture to culture, from person to person. Social determinants of this variability are topics for the sociology of knowledge, as are the social determinants of "competence" in a given audience.

CHAPTER 2 □□

Political Beliefs and
Motivations for
Seeking Office

Although the racial identification of given officials as "Black Americans" is important as a measure of the demographic representativeness of government, the ideological identification of Black officials (and non-Blacks, as well) with the strivings of Black people is essential for ideological representativeness. After all, what goes on inside an official's head may do more than his or her outside appearance to determine how the duties and rights of office are actually carried out. In our interviews, some Black officials made clear the importance they attached to such matters:

If those people are not Black who are elected but only dark in color, then it won't mean much difference to the Black community. After all, what does it matter if a man has natural hair but a processed mind? It doesn't really mean too much. It just means that we have a Black there. He doesn't represent Black people. Black is an attitude of mind, not a color. I know some Black people who are White; I know some White people who are Black. Therefore, when I say Black militants I mean people who are Black in terms of attitude and mind—who are fearless in terms of processing their elective positions with some sort of independence, getting their support and power base from the Black community.

But just what *do* Black elected officials think about issues of general importance to the Black community and to the nation at large? For inclusion in our survey questionnaire, we selected four such issues that seem

17

conceptually related as (1) a possible condition of social action (racial hereditarianism versus non-hereditarianism), (2) a possible means of social action (direct-action versus conventional-action), and (3) possible goals of social action (independence versus integration for Blacks, and political liberalism versus conservatism). Let us examine each of these in greater detail.

Racial Hereditarianism. Our measure of hereditarianism[1] estimates the extent to which officials believed inherited racial traits determine individual and group achievement. The belief that a given trait is inherited is tantamount to defining that trait as an unchangeable *condition* imposed upon social action rather than a controllable *means* employed by social action (ignoring, of course, the developing but still insignificant practical possibilities of direct genetic manipulation). "Hereditarians" would therefore be expected to believe that the potentialities of voluntary human action addressed to social problems of race are more severely limited than would "non-hereditarian" respondents.

It is important to note that our questionnaire avoided any necessary implication of "superiority" or "inferiority" regarding either inherited racial characteristics or performance. For that reason, we prefer the unfortunately cumbersome term "hereditarianism" to the more familiar term "racism." Note also that we speak of "non-hereditarians" rather than "anti-hereditarians" as the opposite of hereditarians because all we know about the former is that they "disagreed" with the hereditarian statement; we do not know what they would have said in its place. Our indicator of hereditarianism, together with the distribution of responses to it, is shown in Table 2.1. The question was asked of White as well as Black officials, and the percentages on this variable are directly comparable across all respondent categories.

Table 2.1. Question Used as Indicator of Hereditarianism (versus Non-Hereditarianism): "Inherited racial characteristics play more of a part in the achievement of individuals and groups than is generally thought."[a] (Percent)

Strongly Agree	Agree	No Opinion	Disagree	Strongly Disagree	Total
		Black Officials			
11	28	11	27	23	100 (759)
		White Officials			
6	36	16	32	9	100 (467)

a Item borrowed from Kerlinger (1967). See Robinson et al. (1968:101).

1 See footnote a in Table 2.5 for information about how this index was constructed.

The chief findings of the table are (1) although White officials were expectedly more hereditarian than were Black officials, the difference was surprisingly slight; and (2) the more striking difference that was associated with race of official lay in the greater tendency of Black officials to take extreme (e.g., "Strongly Agree") positions—both for and against hereditarianism. Later in this chapter we will show evidence suggesting that whereas White officials might be described as being either non-hereditarians or White-supremacist hereditarians (i.e., believers in the hereditary superiority of Whites over Blacks), Black officials may conceivably have fallen into three groups: Black-supremacist hereditarians, White-supremacist hereditarians, and non-hereditarians. Thus, both the unexpectedly small race-related difference in hereditarianism and the equally unexpected tendency of Black officials to take the extreme pro-hereditarian position probably reflected a special, pro-hereditarian, but anti-White supremacist, ideological component among Black officials.

Direct-Action versus Conventional-Action. Our second ideological measure assesses the relative appropriateness of two broad categories of social action *means*, and we call this our index of preference for direct-action (versus conventional-action). Here we intended to acknowledge division of beliefs in the Black community regarding the type of activities that ought to be employed to accomplish social progress for the Black community, whatever may be the conditions of that progress and however its goals may be defined. These questions were asked of Black officials only.

In Table 2.2 we find that over 90 percent of Black officials indicated that conventional means, including court action, legislation, petitions, and delegations, were "Very Important" or "Fairly Important" in achieving progress for Blacks in America. When it is recalled that our respondents were all voluntarily, and probably with some moral commitment, engaged in one type of conventional means of social action—namely, institutionalized government—this strong preference is not surprising. But what seems more noteworthy are the facts that 55 percent indicated that mass public demonstrations, sit-ins, marches, etc., were "Very Important" or "Fairly Important" and 21 percent subscribed to "the use of violence when peaceful methods fail." In our interviews, we repeatedly heard praises for militancy:

> There's a guy whom I admire tremendously. We can speak in terms of H. Rap Brown. I remember not too long ago if a Black woman would walk the street or a Black man, they would say, "Boy, get out in the street. Get off the sidewalk and into the street." This was a

Table 2.2. Questions[a] Used in Index of Preference for Direct-Action (versus Conventional-Action): "In your opinion, how important is each of the following in achieving real progress for Blacks in America?" (Percent)

	Very Important	Fairly Important	Not too Important	Not Important at All	Total
			Black Officials		
Mass public demonstrations, sit-ins, marches, etc.	16	39	30	15	100 (739)
The use of violence when peaceful methods fail	7	14	22	57	100 (712)
Court actions and legislation[b]	89	10	1	—	100 (758)
Petitions and delegations[b]	65	26	8	2	100 (743)

[a] The idea for these questions came from Conyers, et al. (1968), Harris (1970), and Edgar G. Epps (personal communication).

[b] Reverse scored.

way of life. But I think of the joke I heard recently: There was a Black man at the airport; there was also a White man standing very close next to him. The White man very reluctantly and very politely asked the Black man, "Are you a member of the Black Panther Party?" The Black man said, "No." "Are you a member of the NAACP?" and he said, "No." He said, "Are you a member of CORE?" and he said, "No." The Black man, after a series of these questions asked, "Why do you want to know this?" And the White man then said, "Well I wanted to ask you if you would please get off my foot." This is what I mean by the effect of militancy.

*

A good riot is when the Blacks got up and armed and said, "Look; we've had enough! We want to move out of the rat-infested dwellings of the ghetto," and they decided to burn the ghetto. Blacks have to be militant. Now I don't mean burning, looting, killing, and this type of thing. That to me has served its purpose. But we have to be militant in standing up for what we feel is right. We have to be much more independent.

*

The younger Black groups and the militant Black groups are causing even the older Blacks to see more clearly the picture of inequities that we've got in the country.

NOTE: The single asterisk is used throughout this book to separate quotations from different informants.

*

I don't believe that people who have power voluntarily give up enough of it to make a difference in what they have. So I think that whatever happens people have to be forced to make a change.

*

We have been brainwashed to the point where we believe Columbus discovered America. And if he did, you know the question was asked, "What were all those Indians doing here when he discovered it?" We then are told that we were not anarchists when we took this country from the British or from the Indians. We stole it from the Indians, but we were not anarchists when we took it from the British; we were revolutionaries. And, of course, to me the definition of anarchy or revolution is if you lose, it's a riot, and if you win, it's a revolution.

One Black official outside the South reported:

I was talking with my city manager, and he's from Florida, and he told me that once he asked [a White city official in that state] for a job as assistant city manager, and [the official] told him "No." But he said, "If I ever need you I'll call you." Got a little hot down there and he called him and said, "Need you now, because we need a Black image for the Blacks." So, Whites are willing to help Blacks to get on.

With specific reference to violence, officials said:

When the country reaches a point where it refuses, through peaceful, legitimate, and legislative means, to share what the country has with those that have made the contribution, then I suppose that one has to see what forces are available in order to bring about a change since the political avenue has explored it and been unsuccessful.

*

There's an outside chance that you may have a violent revolution in this country, to the extent that we continue to close the democratic avenues for change by passing such laws as pre-trial detention, for example, by providing concentration camps, by passing laws saying that if you go across state lines to make a speech and a riot results, then you are responsible for the riot. That kind of thing only tends to dry up avenues for peaceful change, and you don't leave people any choice but to fight. To that extent, you're really causing a revolution.

Still another tempered his prediction of future violence with an appreciation of the anti-polarizing and anti-violence tendencies of social and cultural pluralism:

> I'm not naive enough not to believe that there won't be some type of violence. There always has been; I don't know why we're any different. You know if you trace the world—trace the history for two thousand years—every race that has really been free has been free through violence. But every revolution that I have ever heard of has been within the same ethnic group, and the only difference was political or religious philosophy. It's hard to have revolution in a country where there's every ethnic group and various religions and various philosophies. It's hard to get that many people together against or for any one thing.

On the other hand, one official said:

> Young people are not going to find solutions to their problems in the streets. We've all found this out from the 60's and 70's with all the riots and different things that have gone on across the country. There is nothing to be found in the street but catastrophe and violence and destruction of lives and property.

Black Independence versus Integration. Among ideological attitudes, we also chose to examine two types of social action *goals:* those bearing on relations between races and those bearing on relations between classes. Regarding the first, we constructed an index of support for Black independence (versus integrationism),[2] designed to assess relative commitment to a collective independence of Black Americans that is explicitly based on racial identity or to an individual option of Black Americans that explicitly ignores racial identity. The distributions of responses to questions used in constructing this index are presented in Table 2.3. Note that there were pairs of questions designed to assess support for independence versus integration in business, in education, and in politics and government. Note also that those questions refer only to independence or integration at the institutional level; none of them refers to independence or integration at more micro-social levels (i.e., between individuals) or macro-social levels (i.e., between communities, between nations, or between groups of nations). The questions employed in this index were asked of Black officials only.

The interviews cast considerable light on the way Black officials

---

2 See footnote a in Table 2.5.

themselves viewed the terms "separation" (or, as we prefer to call it here, "independence")[3] and "integration." In general, there seems to have been strong opposition to separation between Black and White nations, but equally strong support for a separateness of the Black community that would combine outside aid with inside control and that would involve coalitions among several such administratively independent communities of different racial, ethnic, religious, and other backgrounds. One official expressed it this way:

> I reject the idea of separatism. That is, in the sense of Black people being totally apart and separate to themselves, forming a different nation. I don't know if integration in this country in the sense in which it was idealistically envisioned originally will ever occur. But I do believe that there is a chance for some kind of racial reconciliation. There is a chance at least for a multi-racial society based on racial equality which, by the way, presupposes groups having power to control their lives and their destinies.

Another said:

> I think separation is a healthy tool in certain respects. I don't think that there's any viability in the idea of a separate Black nation in this country. I think we constitute a psychological-cultural nation already, and I think we have to employ separatism economically, that is shop and deal with Black firms. But I don't think we're going to be able to set up a separate state, politically.

Another defended Black colleges, in particular:

> I think that Black separation and integration are two terms that somebody has to find a synthesis for. I would not say that I am a separatist, and I would not say that I am an integrationist. I would say though, that there is merit in the idea of separatism in certain areas. I think that there are certain areas that ought to be completely separatist or perhaps even completely integrated. For example Black colleges, which made it possible for many of our present-day Black leaders to become sufficiently well-qualified to provide some leadership. These people could not have been around had it not been for Black colleges. And I think that there will always be a need for them.

---

[3] We prefer the term "independence" to "separation," because the former is less restrictive than the latter (i.e., physical separation may or may not be required for, or a characteristic of, independence), and we do not know how much importance our respondents assigned to such separation as against other aspects of independence.

And another urged independent Black development, especially in the business entrepreneurial life of the United States.

> You know, we have got to be able to have buildings like the one we are sitting in here. We have got to be able to build them. We've got to be able to finance them, and if we don't get a part of this, then someone's going to have to turn this thing around another way. We've turned things around socially. Now we're going to have to turn things around economically.

On the other hand, an official in a southern state asked:

> Would it be better for Negroes to be all by themselves wrestling with the problems of housing, ghettos, slums and education and jobs? Would they do better by themselves than they would do fighting this terrible racial situation within the American capitalistic system? Will separatism abolish slums and ghettos? Will it provide jobs for every man who is able to work? Will it provide better schools? If separatism can answer these questions in the affirmative, then I might go along with it. But I don't see that the separatist movement has any program that's going to eliminate the basic ills confronting Black people today.

And another argued that electorates should not refer to race at all.

> One should not have to be in a situation where one is in a total Black community and be forced into having to elect a Black official to represent you, because there are no White persons available. Those who can do the most for all people with regard to economic process should be the ones who are elected.

But the southern official quoted above expressed doubts about the practicability (though none about the desirability) of such integration.

> I have always shied away from the word "integration" because integration to me means a perfect state, which I don't visualize in my lifetime or hardly anybody else's, where all class and all race would be abolished. And it would be just as easy for a Black man to get ahead as it is for a White man to get ahead. It would be just as easy for the low class man to move upward as for the so-called upper class. So I would like to use the word "desegregation." The integrated society is a long, long way off.

And as this latter statement indicates, the definitions of "separatism" and "integrationism" were questions on which our informants recognized little agreement. One official denied the applicability of the term "sep-aratism" to caucusing among Blacks within a given organization.

I don't consider that separatism. It's like getting together in your own family, ironing out your family problems to meet the real prob-lems of the society.

And another commented on the White community's tendency to evaluate an official who gives special attention to his or her own constit-uency positively, if that constituency is White, but negatively if it is Black.

In our society when you move effectively to do something for your people or the constituency that elects you, which happens to be Black, then often the White person says this is racist. But when they practice the same thing, they call it Americanism; and when we do it, they say it's racism. And this, of course, is not true.

Regarding the importance of coalitions between the Black commu-nity and others, one official declared:

You have to have control of your own destiny in your own hands, and then you have to make alliances with other groups who are also victims of the system and who have a vested interest in radical change. You have several identifiable groups that are demanding change—you have the young people, you have the cities, the cam-puses, the Black community, you have the returning Vietnam vets who face unemployment and disdain, you have the whole peace movement, and, I believe, the Women's Lib Movement. Once they take the struggle out of the bedroom into the streets where it be-longs, a potential part of a coalition would turn this country around.

And another asked:

Do Black folks live next to other poor folks, who happen to be Puer-to Rican, or Mexican, or Indian, or Chinese? Is it possible for these two groups collectively to support a candidate and to reach a coali-tion? I think that you will be seeing more and more elected officials representing minority people throughout the United States. The de-gree to which they can form other coalitions where minorities can influence the majority would depend on the fears of these minority groups in working with each other.

This official generalized further:

I think soon we'll be able to convince our other ethnic brothers (Ital-ian-American or Polish-American, or to a certain extent, the Irish-

American), that he, too, has not been included in the American dream. A free college education could be considered to be a minority problem and certainly we would be advocating support for it. But we know that we can get support from the Italian-American, the Irish-American, the Jewish-American as he, too, attempts to move further up that economic ladder.

Interestingly, the groups mentioned as likely partners in coalitions with the Black community did not often include labor unions. One official said:

Labor unions, traditionally the friends of Blacks, have become so institutionalized that they now have a vested part of the status quo. They don't care about unemployment. They don't care about organizing the unorganized because all of the lucrative fields of labor organization have already been covered, so the domestics are not a concern of theirs. They're concerned about maintaining benefits, raising unemployment compensation benefits for their workers who are laid off. They're becoming conservative.

Now it should be clear that, as one of the above informants indicated, community independence logically requires persistent communities. Therefore, it should come as no surprise that Black officials whom we interviewed vigorously opposed any shrinkage of the Black community, whether accomplished through political means or birth control programs. Although Black officials' attitudes toward both will be examined more closely later, it may be useful to present a few relevant interview statements here as well. One informant was especially critical of urban renewal:

There is no doubt that [urban renewal] was an attempt to break up concentration of Black political power. Because of the fact that these people had been in the same community for years, they developed a certain unity and sophistication that does not exist in communities consisting of strangers. But over and above that, there are many Black communities across our country that have been of some long development; developed a type of cohesion that might be likened to a small town. And when you recklessly bulldoze such a community, you're playing social havoc with the lives of these people who are scattered all across the city; the Black population becomes a group of strangers. It is, therefore, socially and politically continually kept off balance. Black people never have a chance to sink roots to develop permanent relationships with each other; and as a consequence, they don't develop the social stability that, in my opinion, is basic to a healthy community; nor can they organize the sophistication that is necessary to protect their interests in the political field.

Another opposed metropolitan government[4] plans:

I believe right in my city the future of Black elected officials is pretty dim, because now they're trying to go to uni-gov.

Q: That tends to dilute the Black vote?

A: That's right. It would make all the Black councilmen run at large.

Q. On the county level or something like this?

A: Yes, on the county level, and we don't have any Black people living in the county. And we only constitute 10 percent of the 180,000 people in the city.

One official tentatively identified social policies that advocate birth control as threats to the Black community:

Frankly, I'm very conflicted in my own mind about this, but there is a great deal to be said about the connection between population control of Black people and genocide. I really wonder in my own mind sometimes if maybe I am not becoming paranoid or maybe, on the other hand, if I am not becoming much more aware than ever I have been before of the forces affecting the lives of Black people. And that instead of becoming paranoid what I am really doing is peeping the hole cards, so to speak, of those who in fact have very devious schemes to control and to manipulate.

We have already quoted references to two areas of social life, higher education and business entrepreneurship, in which officials expressed interest in Black independence. Table 2.3 presents survey data regarding other areas as well, and it may be seen here that although 97 percent of Black officials indicated a judgment that "more Black-owned businesses" were either "Very Important" or "Fairly Important" in "achieving real progress for Blacks in America," only 64 percent similarly associated themselves with "more Black-controlled schools and universities" and only 24 percent associated themselves with "formation of an independent all-Black political party." This suggests that to Black officials, racially independent development in business and economics was a more important goal than independent development in education, and the latter was more important than independent development in politics and government. But

---

[4] Regarding metropolitan government and the Black community, see Hatcher (1969), Sloan and French (1971), and Johnson (1972).

we also find that the same order prevails with respect to the integrationist side of each of the preceding questions. That is, 93 percent, 88 percent, and 74 percent of our respondents indicated that racially integrated development in the areas of business, education, and politics and government, respectively, was important.

Table 2.3. Questions[a] Used in Index of Preference for Black Independence (versus Integration): "In your opinion, how important is each of the following in achieving real progress for Blacks in America? (Percent)

| | Black Officials | | | | |
	Very Important	Fairly Important	Not too Important	Not Important at All	Total
More Black-owned businesses	86	11	3	—	100 (781)
More Black partners, directors, managers, etc., of White businesses[b]	71	22	6	1	100 (765)
More Black-controlled schools and universities	27	37	29	8	100 (748)
Complete racial integration in schools and universities[b]	70	18	9	2	100 (733)
Formation of an independent all-Black political party	9	15	31	45	100 (735)
Working through the established party structure[b]	59	25	11	5	100 (746)

[a] The idea for these questions came from Harris (1970).

[b] Reverse scored.

Considering the independence and integration sides of these questions together, our data thus appear to represent a rank-ordering of the importance assigned to these various walks of life with respect to Black social progress. In other words, the fact that some 97 percent of Black officials said that more independently Black-owned business was an important goal and that 93 percent of Black officials said that more integrated Black partners, directors, managers, etc., of predominantly White businesses was also important probably means that the officials believed that *something*—whether oriented toward independence or integration or both —has to be done in the field of business, and that action in this field should take priority over the other two fields.

In an interview, one official expressed this priority by saying:

If you want to improve the quality of life of people, to me, the economic structure is the best way to do it. I have to use the political avenue in trying to rebuild that structure.

Another contrasted the value of economic and political advances:

I don't personally think that Blacks progressing as elected officials will be the most important thing in the role of Black people in years to come. White America is not very concerned about any particular offices in the country that a Black man might attain, even the higher offices, such as president and vice-president. These offices do not necessarily control the prosperity of this country. I think it's controlled by the almighty dollar and on streets like Wall Street. And until such time as Blacks do have some input and inroads into this segment of American life, certainly we won't prosper.

But another disagreed with this view:

I don't believe that economic power is the fundamental or the primary basis for change so far as Black people are concerned. If we are talking about enough money to change the lives of the masses of Black people, then we're talking about massive amounts that just simply are not going to be cut loose by those who have it. I think the most viable means is through politics at this time. That's because, it's very simple—if we have two votes and they have one, we win. The thing that I believe now, is that we must in fact redefine the word "we." The word "we" has got to include liberal Whites, poor Whites, and other minorities in this country.

Economic dependence was linked to urban violence.

No one that "has" wants a physical confrontation; but if you have nothing, you have nothing to lose. You don't find those Blacks in the community who own a store or own the co-op, or own the building, out there setting fires.

While a fourth cautioned:

If you are going to drive this Black capitalism to the point that you do not want to be employed by anything that is White capitalistic, then it's doomed.

Table 2.3, while pointing out the general salience of business and economics, also indicates some notable variations among fields with respect to the support given to Black independence and integration. Thus, the fact that 86 percent of Black officials gave the answer most favorable to independence in the field of business, while only 71 percent gave the most integrationist answer, indicates that these respondents as a group were more strongly oriented toward independence than integration with regard to business. But the reverse was true in the other two fields; 27 percent gave the answer most favorable to independence in the field of education, while 70 percent gave the most integrationist answer; 9 percent gave the answer most favorable to independence with respect to politics-government, and 59 percent gave the most integrationist answer in this field. This last finding probably reflects the strong emphasis on within-party coalition politics mentioned earlier, as well as the between-party Black solidarity that seems expressed in one respondent's feeling that once Black Republicans "make the demands that Black Democrats have made on their party, they're going to receive support from all over."

Political Liberalism versus Conservatism. Finally, in an attempt to assess class-relevant social goals, we constructed an index of liberalism (versus conservatism).[5] Questions for this index were asked of all respondents.

A consistently stronger liberal tendency on the part of Black officials than on the part of White officials is revealed in Table 2.4. One interviewed Black official expressed his analysis of American social structure in the following terms:

> The "people" are not controlling America, but seventy families are controlling America and the destinies of over three billion people that cover the earth's surface. Young people are destroying this. They're saying that we are all one, because segregation has been a means by which these seventy families could do this. They could take a poor white in the South and a Negro in the South who are in the same bag and say, "you're not as good as we are, but you're better than he is." But now both of them are finding that it is not a matter of better or not better. Economically, they're both in the same bag, and no matter how well you shake it up, they come out the same way. But together they can extract some of the economic power that the seventy families control.

But the same official also said:

> If everybody owns everything, nobody will take care of anything. There has to be individualism. We can think and talk about masses,

---

[5] See footnote a in Table 2.5.

Table 2.4. Questions[a] Used in Index of Liberalism (versus Conservatism):
"Below is a checklist of statements dealing with contemporary values and
issues. Please check whether you strongly agree, agree, disagree, strongly
disagree, or have no opinion about each statement." (Percent)

	Strongly Agree	Agree	No Opinion	Disagree	Strongly Disagree	Total
In recent times, this country has moved dangerously close to socialism.[b]						
Black officials	11	31	17	31	11	100 (756)
White officials	28	38	7	22	6	100 (469)
In recent times, this country has moved dangerously close to fascism.						
Black officials	12	24	24	32	8	100 (741)
White officials	4	14	16	51	15	100 (451)
A first consideration of any society is the protection of property rights.[b]						
Black officials	15	22	6	34	24	100 (766)
White officials	18	32	5	37	8	100 (468)
True democracy is limited in the United States because of the special privileges enjoyed by business and industry.						
Black officials	25	45	8	19	3	100 (759)
White officials	4	22	9	50	15	100 (468)
There are too many professors in our colleges and universities who are radical in their social and political beliefs.[b]						
Black officials	9	15	20	41	15	100 (766)
White officials	18	39	11	25	6	100 (472)
It is the responsibility of the entire society, through its government, to guarantee everyone adequate housing, income, and leisure.						
Black officials	44	32	5	16	2	100 (767)
White officials	8	22	4	44	22	100 (470)

[a] The first two questions are modified versions of a question devised by Selznick and Steinberg (1966) and reported in Robinson et al. (1968:93). The third, fourth and fifth questions come from Kerlinger (1967), and the sixth question comes from Adorno et al. (1950). See Robinson et al. (1968:100, 101, 110).

[b] Reverse scored.

but we have to actually apply the individualistic process. But we've got to make sure that the masses have an opportunity. Now, if you don't take it, it's your own business—whether you're White or Black.

Our survey data show that some 70 percent of Black officials, but only 26 percent of White officials, agreed that "true democracy is limited in the United States because of the special privileges enjoyed by business and industry." And whereas 56 percent of Black officials disagreed that "there are too many professors in our colleges and universities who are radical in their social and political beliefs," only 31 percent of White officials disagreed with that statement. In order to conserve our case base, given such wide racial discrepancies, we dichotomized the liberalism index at its race-specific medians. The frequently higher liberal percentages among White officials than Black officials is an artifact of this dichotomization (see, for example, Table 2.5), and such percentages are therefore not comparable across race in this study.

Table 2.5 presents the distribution of responses on all four of the ideology measures, controlling for region. Note that the only wide discrepancies between regions occur in liberalism, with the southern officials (both Black and White) showing lower levels than northern officials. It is also noteworthy that support for Black independence was somewhat more widespread among southern than northern Black officials (another finding to which we will give more attention later), and that a preference for direct-action was more widespread among northern than southern Black officials.

Relationships among Ideologies

Now, in view of the conceptual relationships among these ideologies (i.e., as possible conditions, means, and goals of social action) that we mentioned earlier, let us see how they were empirically related to each other. As one would expect, Table 2.6 shows, in both regions, positive associations between independence goals and direct-action means (those who favored independence tended to favor direct-action; integrationists tended to favor conventional-action). The associations of direct-action with independence, however, are stronger than with liberalism. In thinking about these findings, consider that associations between a given means and several possible goals are open to at least three different interpretations. In the first two interpretations, the means is viewed as a cost to be expended rationally, but for a *value* gained in the first interpretation and for a *price* demanded in the second interpretation. In other words, re-

Table 2.5. Ideology Indexes, by Region (Percent)[a]

	South	North
	Black Officials	
Hereditarianism	41 (314)	36 (423)
Direct-action	51 (319)	56 (427)
Independence	59 (324)	51 (430)
Liberalism	31 (327)	54 (427)
	White Officials	
Hereditarianism	47 (208)	38 (253)
Liberalism	50 (209)	67 (251)

[a] The Indexes of Direct-Action (versus Conventional-Action) and of Independence (versus Integration) were constructed by scoring each "Very Important" response as 4, each "Fairly Important" response as 3, each "Not too Important" response as 2, and each "Not Important at All" response as 1 (except, of course, in the case of responses that were reverse scored). A respondent's index value was the simple sum of his or her scores across the questions used in the indexes. Missing scores were supplied by substituting the mean of scores on index questions answered by that respondent, provided that at least two questions had been answered. Index values were then coded "High" or "Low" with respect to the median of such values. The same procedure was followed for the Index of Liberalism (versus Conservatism), except that "Strongly Agree" responses were scored 5 and so on.

The most relevant data for each index are as follows. Index of Direct-Action (versus Conventional-Action): range 4–16, median = 6; Index of Independence (versus Integration): range 6–24, median = 12; Index of Liberalism (versus Conservatism) for Black officials: range 6–30, median = 20; for White officials: range 6–29, median = 14. The higher "Liberal" percentages among White officials than among Black officials in the table is an artifact of this race-specific dichotomization; percentages "Liberal" are therefore not comparable across race in this study.

The Hereditarianism indicator was dichotomized for both Black and White respondents by grouping "Strongly Agree" and "Agree" responses together as "High" versus all other responses grouped together as "Low."

In order to facilitate reading this table: the first cell indicates that 41 percent of the 314 southern Black officials answering were scored "High" on hereditarianism.

spondents' willingness to use a given means in pursuit of a given goal may indicate how *good* they think the attainment of the goal would be, or it may indicate their estimates of how *difficult* that attainment would be.

Assuming that a direct-action means to any goal risks greater costs to the user than does conventional-action, Table 2.6 suggests that to Black officials (1) both independence and liberalism were goals regarded as more difficult to attain, and/or as more highly valued, than were integration and conservatism, but (2) independence was thought to be even more difficult to attain, and/or more highly valued, than was liberalism.

In the third possible interpretation of associations between given means and given goals, a particular means may be morally, rather than

Table 2.6. Associations among Ideological Variables (Yule's Q)[a]

	South			North		
	Direct-Action	Inde-pendence	Liberalism	Direct-Action	Inde-pendence	Liberalism
			Black Officials			
Hereditarianism	.09[b]	.28	—.40	—.03	.03	—.47
Direct-Action		.48	.33		.51	.23
Independence			.16			.10
			White Officials			
Hereditarianism			—.73			—.47

[a] See Goodman and Kruskal (1954).

[b] Whenever a Q coefficient is cited, it was computed from a two-by-two table in which no expected cell frequency was less than five; usually, these frequencies were much greater than five.

rationally, connected to a particular goal, and together they form a single attitude set. For example, to some persons, direct-action (or conventional-action) may be thought of as the only morally appropriate means for a given goal, regardless of how difficult that goal may be to attain and regardless of how highly valued it may be. In extreme cases of this kind, means and ends justify each other; neither can be replaced: Goals and means are one process. With respect to this alternative, the data of Table 2.6 permit us only to conclude that if direct-action means were in fact goal-related in this normative sense, then, among Black officials, such means were made more strongly obligatory by independence goals than by liberal goals (and conventional-action means were made more obligatory by integrationist than by conservative goals).

Hereditarianism as a Condition Imposed on Social Action. Now, let us inquire about the role of hereditarianism as a possible mediator between social goals and social means. In other words, assuming that an official had already adopted particular goals of social action, did a belief in racial hereditarianism as an imposed condition of social action affect his or her choice of means?

The first noteworthy findings in this connection are the negative associations in Table 2.6 of liberalism with hereditarianism and the positive associations of independence with hereditarianism—the latter being especially true inside the South. Thus, socioeconomic "conservatives" and racial "radicals" seem to have found the hereditarian assumption congenial (or at least not uncongenial), while liberals and integrationists definitely did not.

Tables 2.7 and 2.8, however, suggest that hereditarianism played different ideological roles among liberals and proponents of independence, and different roles inside and outside the South. It seems clear that outside the South belief in the bearing of racial inheritance on achievement exerted very little influence over Black officials' choices of means; what mattered most were social goals (i.e., we find that the choice of direct-action by liberals, conservatives, proponents of independence, and integrationists was relatively undifferentiated by their views on hereditarianism).

Table 2.7. Percent Preferring Direct-Action by Liberalism and Hereditarianism[a]

| | Black Officials | | | |
| | South | | North | |
	Liberal	Conservative	Liberal	Conservative
Hereditarianism	50 (26)	53 (101)	65 (57)	48 (94)
Non-Hereditarianism	68 (71)	39 (112)	59 (171)	50 (101)

[a] The first cell indicates that 50 percent of southern, liberal, hereditarian Black officials preferred direct-action.

Table 2.8. Percent Preferring Direct-Action, by Independence and Hereditarianism[a]

| | Black Officials | | | |
| | South | | North | |
	Independence	Integration	Independence	Integration
Hereditarianism	64	31	67	41
Non-Hereditarianism	60	39	68	43

[a] In order to facilitate reading this table (and all subsequent tables of equal or greater complexity), we omit the exact frequencies on which the percentages in it are based. We will, however, indicate the smallest and the largest base found in each table. In this table, the smallest base is 42; the largest is 137. The first cell indicates that 64 percent of southern, Black officials who preferred Black independence and who were hereditarian preferred direct-action.

But inside the South, where hereditarianism has been more explicitly a political issue, the picture is different. Here liberals tended to prefer direct-action more often if they were non-hereditarian than if they were hereditarian (Table 2.7), while advocates of independence tended slightly more toward direct-action if they were hereditarian than if they were non-hereditarian (Table 2.8). Thus, both socioeconomic "conservatives" and racial "radicals" not only seem to have found the hereditarian assumption more acceptable than did their ideological opposites (Table 2.6), but we now see that they were also made more willing by that assumption to adopt the riskier direct-action means of social pressure.

How can such similarities between southern conservatives and southern advocates of independence (and by implication also between liberals and integrationists in that region) be reasonably explained? One possibility is that political conservatism and Black independence were mainly compatible, perhaps even complementary, ideological positions in the sense that they may often have been held by the same person. But Table 2.6 denies that possibility by showing positive associations (though not strong ones) between liberalism and support for independence: At the personal level, liberalism was more compatible with such support than was conservatism.

Perhaps a clue may be found in the fact that the effect of racial hereditarianism on direct-action was much stronger when the social goal was socioeconomic than when it was racial. Indeed, the effect seems to have been only a trace in the latter instance. Although we can only speculate here, this difference suggests the following possibilities.

First, an official could conceivably be just as willing to use direct-action toward independence goals without hereditarian justification as with such justification. Other justifications might serve equally well. These might include a sociocultural hypothesis, sometimes believed to be as existential and inevitable as the hereditarian one but quite different from it—that in order to rectify the effects of long social oppression, oppressed groups must experience independent self-government and develop group self-confidence, while oppressing groups must be confronted by the insubordination, defiance, and secession that those processes imply. But with conservatism, it may be that one advocates "free and unfettered competition" either on the grounds that in this way those who are "naturally superior" will not be hindered in their rise to a dominance which then benefits all, or because, whether "naturally superior" or not, the advocate himself is presently dominant and free competition usually helps perpetuate that dominance. In short, perhaps the only available alternative to the hereditarian justification of conservatism is a narrowly selfish posture that is at least politically inexpedient at present. Thus, whereas socially responsible and politically non-embarrassing alternatives to hereditarian justification may have been available to advocates of independence, no such alternatives may have been available to conservatives. Perhaps as a result, much more of the effect of justification in general was concentrated specifically on hereditarianism among conservatives than among advocates of independence.

A second and contributory explanation arises from the indication of our data that conservative Black officials were tending away from the position of their Black colleagues and toward that of their White colleagues, while proponents of independence probably had the opposite relative tendency, and indeed, they may have leaned more in the direction adopted by their Black colleagues than many of these latter did. Proponents of independence may therefore have been made as militant as they could be by strong social support from their Black colleagues, coupled with their sharp ideological contrast with the White "establishment." For these reasons, believed justification—hereditarian or otherwise—may have had relatively little impact on an already maximally zealous group of Black officials who advocated Black independence. They simply may not have needed such justification.

Conservative Black officials, however, may have responded more dramatically to any justification at all, because they were less likely to receive social support from their Black colleagues, less likely to experience the crusader's zeal because their distinctiveness from the White establishment was less clear, but still not likely to receive adequate approval from the establishment because they were Black.

In summary on this point, Black conservatives may have adopted hereditarian justification (Table 2.6) more, and responded to that justification (Tables 2.7 and 2.8) more, than did proponents of independence for two reasons: (1) Since they may have received less external social support, they had greater need for some sort of internal justification; and (2) since they may have had fewer acceptable alternative justifications, they had a greater investment in the specifically hereditarian one.

Militancy and Community Control. Our interview data reveal further relationships between the advocacies of Black independence and of direct-action and between the former and liberalism. We have already quoted interviews where reference was made to "militancy" in the context of direct-action, and to "community control" in the context of Black independence. But our discussions have risked oversimplified interpretations of the quotations themselves, because the term "militancy," as respondents used it, seems definable as a conditional preference: in favor of direct-action, but only when it is employed toward increased independence for the Black community. The term "community control," as used by our respondents, also seems definable as a conditional preference: in favor of community administrative independence, but only when accompanied by aid from city, county, state, federal, and other extra-community sources. Let us therefore consider some further implications of these two sets of ideas.

Regarding militancy, it is important to reemphasize that Blacks who had voluntarily become duly elected functionaries in a conventional and predominantly White government probably could not easily embrace direct-action and Black independence as the exclusive guides of their own

behavior while holding such office. But on the other hand, their own statements, quoted earlier, indicate that they also did not advocate exclusively
conventional-action means and integrationist goals. Such a dilemma can
be resolved in at least two ways: (1) a *temporal* division of activity (such
that direct-action and independence could be deemed more appropriate in
one time period while conventional-action and integration would be
deemed more appropriate in another), and (2) a *structural* division of
activity (such that it would be deemed appropriate for some Blacks to be
more direct-actionist and more oriented toward independence, while
others, during the same time period, were more conventional-actionist and
integrationist). One informant stressed temporal differentiation.

> Well, I think we've gone through the heights of the Black separat-
> ist movement where the guys go down and create them a Black fo-
> rum and liberate all the folks or separate into a number of states and
> usher all the Black folks into it. I think that the White backlash to
> the Black power movement has subsided, and I think there is begin-
> ning to appear a new breed of person, Black and White, to deal with
> interests that confront us.

Q: Within the structure?

A: . Within the structure of the system, but I think these people will
change the structure of the system.

Others stressed structural differentiation:

> My biggest aid has been the fact that there was a Black community,
> and it always stood as a threat, and it was something that I could al-
> ways refer to. And it has helped to bring Whites around to a more
> equitable point of view whereas if this potential power did not exist,
> I would not be able to work for it too.

*

> There's a large section of the Black community that for a long time
> dismissed politics as irrelevant, and who've been turned off and don't
> look for any viable solution in that direction. These are generally the
> more militant, and in some cases, the more intelligent. Now, we need
> the participation of these people in the political process if the Black
> community is to have its proper type of representation in govern-
> ment.

But each of these two resolutions of the dilemma of militancy in office
presents its distinctive technical problems, and we believe some of these
are reflected in our interviews. Consider the temporal resolution: Its chief

problem is the coordination of activities among the several parts of the system. In other words, for a temporal division of activity to work, the distinctiveness of each time period must be preserved, and therefore different structures have to shift from one phase to another on schedule. When structures become out-of-phase or uncoordinated with one another, a dislocation is likely to be felt. Thus, if a Black official defines a given moment as belonging to one phase while other sectors of the Black community define it as belonging to a different phase, each is apt to feel a dislocation—that the other is either pushing too fast, or lagging behind.

On the other hand, the chief problem generated by the structural resolution is the maintenance of different activities by different parts of the system. That is, in order for a structural division of activity to work, the distinctiveness of each structure in any given time period must be preserved: Different structures have to be allowed (or forced) to do different things at the same time. Thus, when a Black official is following a particular line of activity and other sectors of the Black community call upon him or her to give up that line and follow the one that they are following, or vice versa, each is apt to feel an abrasion—that the other is encroaching, trying to dominate and dictate, or alternatively, that the other is selfishly resisting wise leadership.

Feelings of temporal dislocation and structural abrasion seem to underlie a variety of interview comments. For example, several respondents said their Black constituencies were overdemanding:

> The Black citizen feels that, number one, the Black politician should get things done overnight, immediately—things that have been suffering for want of attention for many many years. Number two, he feels that because this had not been done that the Black officeholder is not adequate to represent them. Number three, he feels that since you've got this Black officeholder up there he is covering up or he is clouding the issues—in other words, if the Black officeholder were not sitting up there where everyone could see him and make things look good, more attention would be given to his problem.

*

> The biggest problem now that I can see in the Black community is that the demands, the problems, have been there all the time but they think they can be solved overnight by having the Black representatives there.

*

> The Black man is called on by his constituency far in excess (generally that is) of what his actual capacity is. He is expected to perform miracles; he is subject to become the object of the frustrations, I

mean the age-old frustrations of Black people who sometimes un-realistically look to him to be able to change overnight the things that have happened.

*

You're a hero to the Black community today if you champion a cause they bring to you—and you do it exactly the way they want it done —and you're a goat tomorrow if you can't see that the thing that they want you to champion is in the best interests of the total com-munity. In other words, you're a "Brother" today, and you're an "Uncle Tom" tomorrow. This is your biggest obstacle in the Black community.

Another was especially aware of the rules of the game of conventional politics.

We sometimes have extremists who do a lot of dreaming about poli-tics, but when you get down to actually playing the game, it's quite real.

Q: Are you suggesting that there are some factions in the Black community who don't understand the nature of compromise, strategy, and so forth?

A: Very definitely so. I think that this has been a hindrance to Black elected officials in the past—they haven't had the ability to look at politics like it is. They haven't adopted the theory that White elected officials have had over the years, and that's that you have to give some and take some.

Others stressed that Black officials in government are bound by conven-tional rules of government that other sectors of the Black community do not comprehend.

I think some people look to the judge and think that "You're one of us, and you can do something for us," and they don't realize that when you administer law you're bound by a set of rules. You have to go by those rules. Then in some instances I felt a little difficulty in those situations because I think the people went away feeling that they didn't get justice, or maybe they go away feeling that one of their own didn't help them or turned his back on them. But after a short time as you try cases everyday, you just reach the point where you go on the facts, you go on the evidence, and you're not actually charged with making decisions. You're charged with seeing that both sides get a fair trial.

And some emphasized their designated role as representatives of the White, as well as of the Black, community: "You cannot consider yourself a Black councilman; you must consider yourself a councilman who happens to be Black. That's all."

> I tried to tell a guy—he was telling me about relating to Blacks—and I told him, I said, I've been knowing I was Black since 1921. I said, because I grew up in a place where I had to know it. When you're telling me about relating to you, I know how to relate to you, and I know what you need. I know your needs as a Black person, period, but I just can't forget about the total population. Well, this is one of my major problems with my group. When I say group, I'm talking about the Blacks. Since we're there, they just say "Turn the city over to us. We need it. We should have had it long ago, and forget them." But because we have been mistreated—and I can't say we haven't—we don't want to go and kill another section. I mean push them on right out of the city. A lot of people don't understand the working of a city. Some people, especially the Blacks, think if you've got public buildings, that you can give it to them. You can't do this. You can't give away city property. We have an old township hall, three stories. And they want to use it for a boys' club, and they think the city can give it, and you can't! The law prohibits such. Then they say: "Well, go and repair it; fix it up, and let us use it." But you can't do this. You get two or three that's interested in helping boys and girls, and they say you're not doing anything for them because you can't give away city property. If we did, we would be neglecting our duty under the laws of the state and the charter of the city.

*

> I think maybe my greatest need is a sense of understanding on the part of my Black constituents, number one—that a Black councilman has to be a councilman for all the people. This is hard, many times, for the Black community to understand and this makes a Black councilman's job much more difficult, and it keeps him walking a very tight rope where the other councilmen can be absolutely at ease because they're not concerned too much about the Black community or how the Black community reacts.

Some informants walked this tightrope with studied balance.

> I represent myself to be a man who will fight for people—that means White and Black people who are oppressed and who are needy, especially. And therefore I never have campaigned with the idea that I will only fight for, and only support Black people.

Another remarked that:

> Everytime I carry the cudgel for the Black community and am real vocal about it, the White community says that I seem to believe that I'm on the council only for the benefit of the Black community when they gave me their votes to represent them just as much.

But others are more explicitly partisan representatives, while propounding a nonpartisan rationale.

> I've said for a long time that I'm not really a representative of the Black community in my hometown or a representative of the White community. I'm a representative of the people, recognizing, however, that one of the biggest problems that we have throughout the country are Black problems. Therefore, as a representative of the people, I've got to attack the problems that are greater, and they have to be the Black problems. I will raise just as much hell in the Black community as I do in the White community in getting this underway.
>
> *
>
> I don't think that in fighting to correct the social problems that plague the Black community, I've been doing a disservice to the rest of the state's community. I consider that in fighting for advancement and for the adjustment of the problems of Black people in our state, I've been fighting in the interest of all the people of the state.

At least one informant, identifying himself as a militant, perceived a widening gap between militants who were not in government office and himself.

> There's an apolitical, anti-political, tendency developing among many militants who regard that even lending aid to this two-party system (at least in their rhetoric) is counterproductive to nation-building time. Calling for "What time is it? It's nation time," produces fantastically different responses in people. In many ways, a lot of the young people are growing critical of people who've been in office. Many of the people who are young now are unaware that I had to fight the establishment to get in. They had heard of nothing but me and my organization; and to them, I represent the establishment if they are not careful to separate the real nature of my political activity.

Thus it would appear that Black officials in our sample had their problems managing their own and their Black constituencies' militancy—in the sense of generating structural coordination as well as temporal coordination between them.

Turning briefly now to "community control"—one official advocated it for the Black community and extended the idea to the White community as well.

> Now, it's my contention that community control is good for White people as well as Black people. In spite of the fact that some White people perceived it as a move for Black power. Certainly it would have been a move for Black power where Blacks happen to be in a majority in a given area, but it will also enhance White power where Whites were in the majority.

However, the same official, when asked, "What is the biggest problem you see as a Black elected official?" emphasized outside aid, in the following quotation. He seems to have epitomized here the link between administration-from-inside-the-community and assistance-from-outside-the-community that comprises "community control" and that seems to have been expressed in the positive associations between independence and liberalism shown by our survey data.

> The biggest problem is racism. The biggest problem is a complete selfishness on the part of (I'm speaking from a state legislative point of view, but I'm sure it's true in Congress as well as in local government)—a perception on the part of most White legislators that any assistance given to the city, for instance, is giving assistance to "ne'er-do-wells" or lazy Black folks looking for a handout. And that's in spite of the fact that the majority of the people who are in [our major city] are still White. When you say [our major city's name], the average White state legislator hears "Black." When you say ADC or welfare, they hear "Black" in spite of the fact that three-quarters of the recipients of welfare in our state are White. When we say "community college," they hear "Black." That is in spite of the fact that only 40 percent of the students at community college are Black. When you say "school system," they hear "Black."

Thus our questionnaire and interview data seem to produce complex pictures of the ideological dispositions and dilemmas experienced by Black elected officials. Further light on these matters will be cast by our next topics—motivations for seeking elective office—especially when we examine their relationships to the ideologies just discussed.

Motivations for Seeking Office

As indicated earlier, we were concerned not only with various facets of officials' political ideologies, but also with their personal motivations for seeking public office. For this latter purpose, we assessed four such possible motivations, which we think of as manifesting two cross-cutting distinctions. The first distinction is between two potential beneficiaries of a given act—oneself and others—and the second distinction is between two possible social sources or recipients of such benefits—a subgroup (including an individual member) of some more inclusive group and the more inclusive group itself. Through this conceptualization, we mean to recognize that officials may be motivated toward gratification of self through gaining acceptance from some group that is the source of that gratification —either a particular subgroup (e.g., an elite, "insiders"), or a more inclusive group (e.g., the "public," the "people"). Similarly, officials may be motivated toward the gratification of others (who thus become the recipients, rather than the sources, of gratification), who constitute a subgroup (e.g., "disadvantaged Americans," "Black Americans") or a more inclusive group (e.g., "Americans"). The distributions of responses on the four relevant questions are shown in Table 2.9.[6]

Table 2.9. Questions[a] Used as Indicator of Motivations: "How important to you personally are the following possible reasons for seeking public office? Please rank them from 1 to 4, counting 1 as 'most important' and 4 as least important.' " (Percent)

	Black Officials Rank					White Officials Rank				
	1st	2nd	3rd	4th	Total	1st	2nd	3rd	4th	Total
A desire to be "on the *inside*"	20	41	32	7	100 (647)	12	27	46	15	100 (383)
A desire to have personal *prestige* and income	4	4	16	76	100 (608)	4	8	19	69	100 (371)
A desire to *correct* social injustices	79	16	3	2	100 (720)	32	40	16	11	100 (400)
A desire to *serve* my country	24	26	30	20	100 (650)	67	20	8	5	100 (442)

a The ideas for these questions came chiefly from Lane (1959:101–114).

It may be seen in Table 2.9 that the crucial difference between Black officials and White officials is the former's strong emphasis on correcting social injustices and the latter's almost equally strong emphasis on serving the country. Note that both of these motivations cast the self in the role of donor rather than recipient of gratification, but one of them implies the identification of an unjustly treated subgroup as recipient, while the other

---

[6] In examining Table 2.9, it should be understood that many respondents gave uncodable answers to the question asked of them—usually by giving two or more alternatives the same or intransitive ranks. This accounts for the drastically reduced case base here and in all subsequent tables in which the motivation variables are involved.

identifies the undifferentiated and more inclusive "country" as recipient. It seems very likely that these motivational differences reflect a stronger tendency of White Americans to see themselves as belonging to this country and this country as belonging to them, while Black Americans tend more to see themselves as strangers here.

In this light, the stronger desire among Black officials than among White to be "on the inside" (61 percent of the former gave this desire first or second rank, while only 39 percent of the latter did) seems immediately understandable: The outsider simply wants "in"—"in" for its own sake, a "piece of the action" no matter what that "action" may be. But there is at least one other possible interpretation, and this arises from the fact that any of the four motivations could easily be conceived as instrumental to the others. Thus, a desire to be "on the inside" might not be an end in itself, but a means for correcting social injustices, serving the country, or gaining personal prestige and income.

One way of assessing this possibility is to examine associations among the motivations. Wherever we find a positive association, a means-end relationship is possible (though by no means necessary), but wherever we find a negative association, no such relationship is logically possible. Note, therefore, the positive association shown in Table 2.10 among Black officials between wanting to be "on the inside" and wanting to correct social injustices. A means-end relationship is therefore possible between these two. In this relationship, logically speaking, either could be means and either could be end. But if correcting social injustices were taken as a means to getting "on the inside," rather than the reverse, an elaborate and implausible duplicity implying demagoguery on the part of our respondents would have to be presumed, without evidence. On this argument, we take the desire to correct social injustices as end, and the desire to be "on the inside" as means.

Table 2.10. Associations among Motivational Variables (Yule's Q)

	South			North		
	Correct	Prestige	Serve	Correct	Prestige	Serve
			Black Officials			
Inside	.32	.25	—.95	.21	.20	—.64
Correct		—.26	—.23		—.34	—.17
Prestige			—.30			—.61
			White Officials			
Inside	—.28	.36	—.02	—.02	.27	—.50
Correct		.18	—.92		—.03	—.89
Prestige			—.29			—.48

Now note that although the desire to be "on the inside" had a positive association among Black officials with the desire to correct social injustices (and thus benefit a subgroup), its associations with the desire to benefit the more inclusive group by serving the country were uniformly negative and strongly so among Black officials. It is as though officials, both Black and White, who were motivated by the desire to help some specific subgroup of the general population, tended to accept the notion that more advantaged and more powerful subgroups (for example, a "power elite," an "establishment") exist and may then have resolved to gain entry to these groups (to get "on the inside") in order to provide that help. But those who were motivated by the less differentiating goal of serving the country may have been repelled by the very idea that an "inside" exists, let alone that they should aspire to join it. In any case, getting "on the inside" was certainly not viewed as a means of serving the country by southern Black officials. But then it should also be observed that the latter desire was negatively associated with every other motivation among both Black and White respondents in the South and North. Consequently, it appears that the desire to serve the country was perhaps naïvely nondiscriminating (in the perceptual sense), but in any case it was quite a different motivation from all the rest.

In that connection, note that the mildly negative association among Black officials between the desires to serve the country and to correct social injustices becomes strongly negative among White officials. It is as though the latter perceived a sharp incompatibility between correcting social injustices and serving the country, and they made their choice; Black officials did not perceive so sharp an incompatibility. To some Black officials at least, correcting social injustices may have been a way of serving the country. This possibility seems to have its complement in the finding that associations between the desires to correct social injustices and to have personal prestige and income are more positive among White respondents than among Black respondents. Thus Black officials were less likely to see a contradiction between serving the country and correcting social injustices, but more likely to see a contradiction between seeking personal prestige and correcting social injustices. The net implication of all this seems to be that Black officials may have been motivated to correct social injustices less for immediately self-gratifying reasons than were White officials.

Now to return to the finding with which the last few pages of the discussion began, namely, the stronger desire of Black officials to be "on the inside." Table 2.10 shows not only that the association between the desire to be "on the inside" and to correct social injustices was positive among Black officials, but also that it was negative among White officials —indicating that the instrumental relation discussed above could not have been as widespread among White as among Black officials. Indeed, our data suggest that among White officials being "on the inside" could have been viewed as instrumental only for self-gratification through gaining personal prestige and income. But clearly, although our data do not indicate that being "on the inside" was instrumental *only* for self-gratification among Black officials, it was probably instrumental *also* for that goal among them—as their positive associations between being "on the inside" and gaining personal prestige and income indicate. Thus we appear to have some confirmation of the consummatory, as well as the instrumental, interpretation of Black officials' stronger desire to be "on the inside" (Table 2.10). To use our earlier phrasing, the outsider seems to have wanted "in" for its own sake (or more exactly, for the sake of the personal self-gratification it could bring) as well as because being "in" could imply more leverage in correcting social injustices and bringing gratification to others.

Our interviews provide some confirmation of the instrumental view of being "on the inside." One official said:

> The most effective fighting is not standing back throwing a jab and then missing by four inches, but by being inside, stepping inside, where when you throw it, it meets.

Another used a different metaphor.

> The fact that we are elected officials gives an entrée into the establishment, and we can use this entrée to consistently prick the conscience of the establishment.

And a third indicated some of the fruits of being "on the inside."

> For years they've gotten around the promotion of Blacks in all of our civil service departments. But now our personnel director is Black. Our human relations director is Black. So we have been relatively successful in the last months in giving Blacks key positions. And my philosophy has always been that you work from the top down, not from the bottom up.

In summary, one official said:

> One of the very rewarding features of holding office is being able to work for the people who put you in there. And being able to change things to benefit the people whom you represent—to change things for the better.

But consider also the opinion of the official who stressed the consummatory or prestige-related aspect of being "on the inside."

> Within the Black community, for example, the social barometers have been for years with educators, with physicians, and maybe with

attorneys; and that has shifted in the recent times because becoming
a Black elected official with executive authority, or judicial authority, or legislative authority—independent these days of a White
overseer—is a new thing. And with this new class, the community
itself has given, in my judgment, a kind of prima donna stature to
Black elected officials. But as the number increases, I think that will
diminish to a degree.

Ideologies and Motivations

Next, let us examine relations between ideologies and motivations:
Did officials having a particular ideological bent have a characteristic pattern of motivation? Our data on this question are presented in Table 2.11.

Table 2.11. Associations among Ideological and Motivational Variables
(Yule's Q)

	South Motivations				North Motivations			
	Inside	Correct	Prestige	Serve	Inside	Correct	Prestige	Serve
				Black Officials				
Hereditarianism	—.17	.06	.26	.08	—.02	—.06	—.25	.19
Direct-Action	.05	—.06	.27	—.07	.30	—.04	.29	—.31
Independence	.01	.05	.26	—.06	.19	.37	.06	—.16
Liberalism	.35	.30	.30	—.55	.24	.36	.27	—.44
				White Officials				
Hereditarianism	—.31	—.88	.14	.87	—.49	—.20	—.71	.66
Liberalism	—.19	.32	.01	—.45	.05	.35	.33	—.55

Reading down the column indicates the ideological correlates of motivations, and reading across the rows indicates the motivational correlates of
ideologies.

We take two interpretational liberties in the following discussion that
deserve brief but explicit mention. The first liberty involves the fact that
one set of data in this discussion refers to our respondents' political ideologies, and the other set refers to their motivations for seeking public office. The liberty we take treats motivations *for seeking office* as though
they were motivations *for* (that is, as reasons for) *holding political ideologies.* We do this on the argument that our motivation data do not represent respondents' assessments of motivations on the part of the typical or
the best or some other abstract Official, but represent assessments of their
own personal, concrete motivations. Our data therefore represent each
respondent's answer to the implied question: "Why do I, as I now am,
with all of my present characteristics, seek public office?" And since some

of these present characteristics are political ideologies, we believe the first liberty we take is reasonable.

The second liberty makes the assumption that motivations and ideologies are causally related, such that one can "sustain" or "reinforce" the other. This does not seem unreasonable either, although our argument is admittedly not a powerful one. There appear to be four logically possible causal assumptions (we say "assumptions" rather than "hypotheses," since we have no way of testing them empirically here): (1) There is no causal (i.e., no direct sustaining) relationship between motivations and ideologies; (2) ideologies sustain motivations, but not the reverse; (3) motivations sustain ideologies, but not the reverse; and (4) motivations and ideologies sustain each other. The fourth assumption is the best for our purposes, but for some of our interpretations, the second alone will suffice, and for others, the third alone will suffice. Only the assumption of no causal connection at all would nullify all of our interpretations, and on purely intuitive grounds we simply reject it as highly unlikely. In other words (although we can offer no empirical support for our belief), it seems likely to us that people who hold given political ideologies will develop personal reasons for seeking office consonant with those ideologies; that people who seek office for given reasons will acquire ideologies consonant with those reasons; and that reasons and ideologies will interact and sustain each other in this way throughout a politician's career.

Given these assumptions, Table 2.11 suggests that in the South the strongest motivational support of belief in independence was the desire for prestige and income, but outside the South its strongest support was the desire to correct social injustices. Although neither association was very strong, the suggestion of these findings is that for some Black officials in the South, advocacy of Black independence may have smacked of personal opportunism—perhaps the projection of a Blacker-than-thou public image whose covert objective may have been personal prestige and income rather than the correction of injustices done to the Black community. Further, we will show in Chapter 5 that in urban areas having relatively small Black populations, southern proponents of Black independence reported that they actually received more election help from the Black community, the White community, their party apparatus, and also the mass media than did southern Black integrationist officials. Under these circumstances, then, the actual "pay-off" in personal prestige (insofar as the latter is indicated by perceived election help) may indeed have been greater for proponents of independence than for proponents of integration. The linkage between belief in independence and the desire for personal prestige and income that Table 2.11 shows therefore does not seem to have expressed an altogether vain hope.

Relationships Between Hereditarianism, Liberalism, Desire to Serve
the Country, and Desire to Correct Social Injustices. Table 2.6 showed
that among Black and White officials in both regions, hereditarianism and
liberalism were negatively associated. But Table 2.11 gives reason to believe that these ideological relationships, sharing the same negative direction, were motivationally sustained in quite different ways among different groups of officials. Figure 2.1 summarizes the relevant data from both
tables (and some from Table 2.10, as well). The following discussion fo-
cuses on this figure.

Figure 2.1. Associations (Yule's Q) of Hereditarianism and Liberalism,
with Motivations

Black Officials

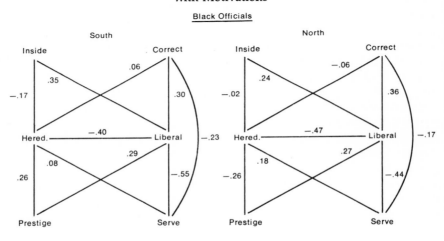

White Officials

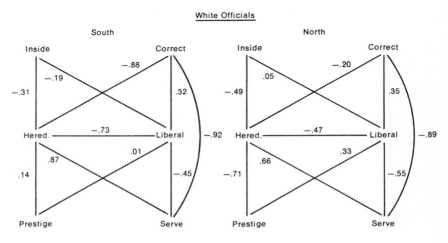

In certain respects, of course, the several negative associations between hereditarianism and leftism were similarly sustained, and these similarities should be noted first, as follows: Negative associations between liberalism and the desire to serve the country are found throughout, as are positive associations between liberalism and the desire to correct social injustices. Also, Black officials and White officials in the South shared positive associations between hereditarianism and the desire for prestige and negative associations between that ideology and the desire to be "on the inside." And northern officials of both races shared positive associations between liberalism and the desire for prestige and negative associations between hereditarianism and the desire to correct social injustices. So much for similarities among the motivational supports of hereditarianism-liberalism relationships.

The differences among these supports are much more revealing. Among southern White officials, there was a strong negative association between hereditarianism and the desire to correct social injustices and an equally strong positive association between hereditarianism and the desire to serve the country. Neither of these associations is found among southern Black officials. It is as though southern White officials found hereditarianism and liberalism incompatible ideologies mainly because (1) the desire to correct social injustices contradicted the significance of inherited and therefore incorrectable racial differences but conformed to liberal notions regarding the ability of people to improve their social system; and (2) the desire to serve the country (presumably including its currently White-supremacist premises) was reinforced by the hereditarian idea that such premises are of cosmic rather than human origin. But among southern Black officials the incompatibility between hereditarianism and liberalism was not as strong as it was among their White counterparts and seems to have been motivationally sustained in a different way. Thus, in addition to the race-related differences just mentioned, it seems significant that southern Black officials reveal a positive association between liberalism and the desire to be "on the inside," whereas the association was negative among southern White officials. One can imagine that southern Black officials found hereditarianism and liberalism incompatible largely because the desire to be "on the inside" was congenial to liberal notions regarding the existence of elite (i.e., ruling, "inside") and subordinate (i.e., ruled, "outside") groups, but not to hereditarian ideas regarding the ineluctability of such distinctions.

When we compare northern Black officials with their White counterparts, we find that although the differences generally followed the same directions as in the South (e.g., the association between the desire to serve the country and hereditarianism was more positive among the Whites), the magnitude of these differences tended to be smaller among non-southern than southern officials. In other words, the differences between Black officials and their White counterparts (in the attitudinal respects shown in Figure 2.1) were of the same kind in both regions, but more pronounced inside than outside the South.

It is also interesting to note that northern White officials shared with their southern White counterparts a negative association between the desire to correct social injustices and hereditarianism, and a positive association between hereditarianism and the desire to serve the country. No such clear pattern is visible among Black officials of either region, where all these associations are slight. One implication of these findings may be that if a White elected official believed "All men are created equal"—that is, without hereditary racial differences that bear on achievement—then he or she was more likely to evaluate certain social distinctions between races (and perhaps between other groups as well) as social *injustices* and more likely to desire to correct these injustices. But if the same official believed in achievement-relevant genetic differences between Blacks and Whites, then he or she was much more likely to be dedicated to preserving invidious social distinctions between Blacks and Whites, and thus dedicated to serving "my country" as presently constituted. In other words, it appears that race was more important to White than to Black officials, both inside and outside the South. This is reflected both in the centrality of White officials' ideas about racial genetic distinctions in relation to social distinctions between races and also by how large a part these officials thought social distinctions between races played in social distinctions of all other kinds—that is, how essential they thought racial distinctions were to the general quality of this nation.

Another set of observations shown in Figure 2.1 are of closely related interest. Notice that with only two minor exceptions, hereditarianism was more strongly associated with all four motivations, and with liberalism, among White officials than among Black officials. Table 4.8 will show that the same racial difference was true of the association between hereditarianism and belief in women's rights. It therefore seems fair to conclude that their acceptance or rejection of racial hereditarianism mattered a great deal to White officials: they felt far more deeply the complementarities and contradictions between hereditarianism and their other beliefs than did Black officials. Thus, despite the small differences in its general distribution among Black and White officials (Table 2.1), hereditarianism seems to have been a central pivot in the belief systems of White officials, but of relatively little importance in those of Black officials.

This racial difference in the salience of racial hereditarianism seems to explain the finding that the association between the desires to serve the country and to correct social injustices were several times more strongly negative among White officials than among Black officials, meaning that White officials were highly unlikely to hold both desires simultaneously. The role of racial hereditarianism in this polarity may be seen among White officials in the contrast between its strongly positive associations with the desire to serve the country and strongly negative associations with the desire to correct social injustices. The only mildly negative association between these two desires among Black officials seems not to have been related to racial hereditarianism at all, but to liberalism.

One final difference related to race of official should be noted in Figure 2.1: The association between liberalism and the desire to be "on the inside" was more positive among Black officials than among White officials of the same region. This may indicate a greater willingness on the part of Black liberals to "join the system and change it from within," and the relatively greater tendency of White liberals to attack the same system from outside.

CHAPTER 3 □□
Personal Background and Social Setting

This chapter will look into how the beliefs and motivations discussed in the preceding chapter are related to personal characteristics, such as the officials' educational attainment, and to social setting characteristics, such as the population size of districts from which officials were elected and the political parties with which officials were affiliated. We want to know, in short, what kinds of officials held various beliefs and motivations and in what kinds of settings these beliefs and motivations were held.

Personal Background

The background variables that concern us here are residence (years lived in the community from which elected), education (number of higher education degrees received), memberships (number of memberships in voluntary organizations), and age.[1] These variables were selected because of our interest in locating Black officials (and comparing them with White officials) along two dimensions that are very likely to be of paramount interest to a politician's constituencies. Briefly, these pertain to the official's familiarity with different kinds of public issues and to different kinds of experience with public issues. In the first dimension, we distinguish be-

---

[1] Two other personal background characteristics play widely different roles in this analysis. One of these, racial identity, is indeed the most important single focus of this study. Sexual identity, the second remaining personal background variable, unfortunately lends itself here to only a brief analysis (see Chapter 4).

tween local and cosmopolitan kinds of public issues, and we employ length of residence as indicator of familiarity with the former and formal education as indicator of familiarity with the latter.[2] We reason that voters, the party organizations, and the mass media are all apt to pay attention to whether a given candidate is from "around here" and therefore personally acquainted with *local* grievances and gratifications or is more systematically (even though vicariously) educated toward *cosmopolitan* interests.

With reference to the second dimension, we rely on the official's age as indicator of duration of experience, because the older official has "been around" *longer*. But we take the official's number of memberships in clubs, lodges, unions, organizations, and other such associations as indicator of range of experience on the assumption that the official who has been more widely involved in the collectively organized affairs of society has "been around" *more*.

In Tables 3.1, 3.2, 3.3, and 3.4, we present the distributions (by race) of residence, education, age, membership. It is evident from these data that on the average, Black officials were slightly more recent residents of their communities than were White officials. Black officials were also somewhat better educated, slightly more prone to join organizations, and slightly older. Translated into the underlying dimensions of which these data are proposed as indicators, this means that (although the differences were not great) Black officials were likely to have more experience with cosmopoli-

---

[2] Our usage of "local" and "cosmopolitan," though derived from Merton's, differs in one major respect from his. Merton argued that formal education was not crucial to the local-cosmopolitan distinction as he saw it in the community called "Rovere": "It is true that the cosmopolitans among our interviewees have received more formal education than the locals. . . . But these differences in . . . educational status do not appear to determine the diverse types of influentials" (1957:402). We, however, assign an importance to formal education equal to that which Merton assigns to residence ("The locals were typically born in Rovere or in its immediate vicinity. . . . The cosmopolitans are typically recent arrivals who have lived in a succession of communities in different parts of the country" [1957:395]). Our grounds derive from Merton's own argument that "the chief criterion for distinguishing the two [types of influentials] is found in their *orientation* toward Rovere. The localite largely confines his interests to this community. . . . [The cosmopolitan type is] oriented significantly to the world outside Rovere, and regards himself as an integral part of that world" (1959:393). We accept this statement as defining the essential difference between locals and cosmopolitans. But we then argue simply that education as well as travel broadens—the one more vicariously, the other more directly. We identify these two types of social experience as giving rise to local and cosmopolitan orientations in two distinct ways. Although among our respondents (see Table 3.6), as among Merton's, recent residents tended to have more years of formal education and were thus cosmopolitan in both ways, other residence-education combinations are possible without nullifying the utility of Merton's local-cosmopolitan distinction.

tan issues but less experience with local issues than their White counterparts and likely also to have more wide-ranging, as well as longer, experience with public issues. (We will see in Chapter 5, however, that Black
officials had won fewer elections and were therefore relative newcomers to
governmental experience.)

Table 3.1. Years Lived in Community from Which Elected (Percent)

Years	Black Officials	White Officials
1–10	16	12
11–20	24	24
21–30	21	17
31–40	14	15
41–50	15	17
51–60	7	11
61–70	3	4
71–80	1	*
Total	100 (783)	100 (476)

* Less than 1 percent.

Table 3.2. Number of Higher Education Degrees Received (Percent)

Number of Degrees	Black Officials	White Officials
None	22	26
One	28	34
Two	41	34
Three	8	6
Four	1	—
Total	100 (612)	100 (381)

Table 3.3. Age (Percent)

Years of Age	Black Officials	White Officials
21–30	3	2
31–40	19	20
41–50	33	36
51–60	30	28
61 and over	16	14
Total	100 (762)	100 (475)

Table 3.4. Number of Memberships in Voluntary Organizations (Percent)

Number of Memberships	Black Officials	White Officials
None	—	3
1–4	35	40
5–9	37	36
10 and over	28	22
Total	100 (777)	100 (460)

Table 3.5. Personal Background Variables, by Race and Region[a]

| | Black Officials | | White Officials | |
Personal Variables	South	North	South	North
Longer residence[b]	61	40	50	45
Higher education[c]	46	52	31	47
Older age[d]	47	45	40	38
More memberships[e]	46	46	34	43

[a] Among Black officials here, the smallest percentage base is 242; the largest is 432. Among White officials here, the smallest percentage base is 161; the largest is 256. The first cell indicates that 61 percent of southern Black officials were long-time residents.

[b] Dichotomized, for all respondents, at > 25 years.

[c] Dichotomized, for all respondents, at > 1 higher education degree.

[d] Dichotomized, for all respondents, at > 49 years.

[e] Dichotomized, for all respondents, at > 5 voluntary associations.

Table 3.5 summarizes the regional distributions of these personal background variables after they have been dichotomized. We find that both Black officials and White officials in the South report having resided in the communities from which they were elected longer than their own-race counterparts in the North, and that northern officials tended to have slightly more education than did their own-race counterparts in the South. Southern officials (especially if they were White) were slightly older than northern officials, and although Black officials do not seem to have varied by region with respect to membership, northern White officials had a slightly higher rate of membership than did southern White officials.

In summing up this table, then, it would appear that southern Black officials were (1) slightly higher than northern Black officials on our measure of local experience and correspondingly lower on our measure of cosmopolitan experience; and (2) slightly higher on our measure of experience duration and either no different or slightly lower on our measure of experience range.

Of greater interest, however, are the ways in which the four personal variables were associated with each other, and these data are shown in Table 3.6. It is important, first, to note a mutual exclusivity between experience with local and cosmopolitan issues as reflected in the consistently negative associations between residence and education among both races of officials, and especially in the South: Officials were likely to have had one but not the other kind of experience. Secondly, note that the associations between memberships and age were less negative (indeed, they were mildly positive outside the South) than those between residence and edu-

Table 3.6. Associations among Personal Background Variables (Yule's Q)

	South			North		
	Education	Age	Memberships	Education	Age	Memberships
			Black Officials			
Residence	—.28	.36	—.54	—.23	.42	.07
Education		.12	.46		.14	.25
Age			—.07			.16
			White Officials			
Residence	—.31	.28	—.13	—.06	.46	.17
Education		.10	.57		.14	.26
Age			—.18			.13

cation, meaning that range and duration of experience were more independent of one another than were the local and cosmopolitan kinds of experience. Thirdly, the associations of age with education and residence were (as expected) positive throughout, although less strongly so in the case of education than of residence—this undoubtedly reflecting the generational upgrading of educational attainment in the United States. Now, however, we come to a finding of greater interest because it will lead to other, less expected, ones later in this analysis. The associations of memberships with education were consistently more positive than those with residence; and the latter associations were even negative in the southern region. In themselves these findings are not surprising, since higher educational attainment is generally associated with joining voluntary associations in the American population at large, and our own data show a negative relationship between education and residence (Table 3.6). But in Chapter 5 we will suggest that memberships carried an additional significance for elected government officials insofar as memberships seem to have functioned in various ways to elicit help in getting elected.

Personal Background and Attitudes

There are several interesting questions bearing on the relationships between the personal background variables introduced here and the attitude variables presented in Chapter 2. For example, was liberalism or hereditarianism, or the desire for personal prestige and income, etc., associated with more education or less education, with recent residence or long-time residence, with a high or low membership rate, with youth or age?

In Table 3.7 we find data relating ideologies to personal background. Perhaps the first item to note here is that throughout all four categories of officials, the more highly educated were also more likely to be liberal and non-hereditarian (the latter relationship is uniformly stronger outside the South). By contrast, the long-time residents (of both regions and both races) were consistently more likely to be conservative and hereditarian. Thus, high cosmopolitan status (education) and high local status (residence) reveal contrasting ideological correlates.

Note that advocacy of Black independence shows not even a moderate association with education or residence in either region, but manifests moderately negative associations in both regions with membership, suggesting that such advocates may have refrained from joining voluntary associations—many of which are likely to have had White participants. Along the same lines, it is noteworthy that integrationists, non-hereditarians, liberals, and those who preferred conventional-action had consistently higher membership rates than did their ideological opposites.

Older Black officials are shown to have been more integrationist, more conservative, and less accepting of direct-action, and although older White officials agreed with their Black counterparts in their relatively more conservative leanings, the former were clearly and consistently more hereditarian than the latter. It is noteworthy in the context of these findings that one younger Black official complained in an interview that:

> My biggest problem has been the Black elected officials who are basically Negroes who had not moved in the 15 or 20 years that they had been here to effectively do anything about the problem that the White liberal did not say was okay. As a result, the record of accomplishment, of course, was damn near nil. That is to say, they are elected by Black votes but are run by the White power structure. So, therefore, when anyone makes an attempt to effectively move to abolish a policy or a law that was created to hurt Black people, they are often the first persons to come up with another idea which will mediate it or effectively kill the amendment, rather than supporting the amendment with all their power and support—because oftentimes, even though you do not have enough votes to pass a law or amendment, if it's brought out, some change then follows as a result of the publicity.

Age Cohort, College, and Ideology. In following up these age-to-ideology relations, let us introduce an additional personal background variable, namely, predominant race of undergraduate college. Since predominantly White colleges have only recently opened their doors to Blacks in any significant numbers, it is possible that this fact underlies the age differences in ideology shown in Table 3.7. Let us therefore ask whether advocacy of Black independence, for example, was more a function of

Table 3.7. Associations Between Personal Background Variables and Ideology Indexes (Yule's Q)

Ideologies	North				South			
	Residence	Education	Age	Memberships	Residence	Education	Age	Memberships
Black Officials								
Hereditarianism	.19	−.17	.10	−.22	.27	−.51	−.03	−.06
Direct-Action	.09	−.07	−.28	−.15	−.20	.01	−.29	−.12
Independence	.01	.07	−.33	−.30	.14	−.11	−.42	−.22
Liberalism	−.33	.26	−.46	.48	−.18	.43	−.21	.02
White Officials								
Hereditarianism	−.22	−.16	.30	−.07	.15	−.33	.23	−.13
Liberalism	.06	.37	−.26	.36	−.20	.22	−.34	.12

school experience (represented, in this case, by the race of one's college student peers) or of age cohort experience. Table 3.8 provides evidence that the latter was clearly primary: Younger Black officials were consistently and markedly more inclined to advocate independence than were older officials. But it also appears that in the older cohort, those who had attended predominantly White colleges (especially in the South) were more inclined in this direction than those who had attended predominantly Black colleges, while there is a slight hint that the reverse might have been true in the younger generation. These findings might conceivably be consequences of the older cohort's more painful experiences with racial dis-

Table 3.8. Percent Having Indicated Attitudes, by Age and Predominant Race of Undergraduate College (Percent)[a]

	South				North			
	Age				Age			
	Younger		Older		Younger		Older	
	Race of College				Race of College			
	Black	White	Black	White	Black	White	Black	White
				Black Officials				
Ideologies								
Hereditarianism	32	50	37	58	29	33	16	35
Direct-Action	55	66	40	44	67	63	50	47
Independence	66	60	37	56	60	59	36	38
Liberalism	48	43	19	26	62	64	54	50
Motivations								
Inside	60	70	73	64	70	66	53	58
Correct	81	79	80	71	82	79	72	77
Prestige	17	15	10	*	30	35	30	37
Serve	51	44	58	64	34	31	38	47
				White Officials[b]				
Ideologies								
Hereditarianism		40		54		46		39
Liberalism		64		46		76		67
Motivations								
Inside		31		41		29		23
Correct		31		21		36		28
Prestige		33		31		28		38
Serve		65		80		55		70

[a] Among Black officials here, the smallest percentage base is 11; the largest is 135. Among White officials here, the smallest percentage base is 42; the largest is 127. The first cell indicates that 32 percent of southern, younger, Black officials who received their undergraduate degrees from predominantly Black colleges were hereditarian.

[b] Only one White official reported having attended a predominantly Black College.

* Base less than 10; too small for percentaging.

crimination on White campuses and of the vigorous attack against off-campus racial discrimination that emerged from Black campuses during the early 1960s.

Table 3.8 indicates that liberalism was also more closely related to age cohort than to race of college, with the younger cohort being more liberal. The limited data on White officials suggest that these findings held for them as well.

In clear and somewhat surprising contrast with beliefs in independence and in liberalism, however, our data show hereditarianism among Black officials was more definitely a function of race of college than of age cohort. Black officials who had attended predominantly White colleges were consistently more hereditarian than those who had attended predominantly Black colleges. Perhaps this is merely a function of the fact that Blacks who attended predominantly White colleges had more first-hand experience with Black-White differences than did Blacks who attended college mostly with other Blacks like themselves. And greater perception of such differences may tend to raise the incidence of any given explanation of them—including the hereditarian one. But perhaps it is also a function of some other experience, whereby Blacks at predominantly White colleges learned the hereditarian explanation in particular. Our data in this study do not permit us to say.

Although, as we have said, the relationship of hereditarianism to race of college was much stronger than that of hereditarianism to age cohort, the latter was visible nonetheless. Thus, younger officials were (with one exception among non-southerners who attended Black colleges) slightly less hereditarian than their seniors. This age effect is seen more clearly among White officials, and one is tempted to conclude that hereditarianism may have been declining somewhat faster over recent years among White respondents than among Black respondents.

A preference for direct-action shows a somewhat more mixed set of relationships than the other ideologies. Younger officials were consistently more direct-actionist, but in the South so were those who attended White colleges, while outside the South such persons were more conventional-actionist.

Personal Background, and Motivation. Returning now to our main line of analysis and turning to the associations of the motivation variables with the personal background variables, Table 3.9 provides our data. In this table we find that, with partial exceptions among White officials, education and residence tended to be related in opposite ways to the desire to correct social injustices and to the desire to serve the country, respectively.

Table 3.9. Associations Between Personal Background Variables and Motivation Variables (Yule's Q)

| Motivations | South | | | | North | | | |
	Residence	Education	Age	Memberships	Residence	Education	Age	Memberships
					Black Officials			
Inside	−.21	.09	.06	.21	−.26	.00	.22	.00
Correct	−.06	.25	−.13	.11	−.03	.14	−.14	−.04
Prestige	.07	.04	−.22	−.14	.19	.11	.00	−.11
Serve	.18	−.28	.24	−.40	.02	−.31	.25	−.04
					White Officials			
Inside	.13	−.20	.14	.04	−.08	−.06	−.30	−.37
Correct	.16	.23	−.06	−.16	.00	.16	−.10	.06
Prestige	−.02	.30	.07	.24	−.10	.30	.31	−.08
Serve	.05	−.32	.23	.20	.17	−.08	.26	.00

Thus education generally tended to support the desire to correct social injustices but to suppress the desire to serve the country. Although the magnitude of the coefficients is generally less for residence, the latter seems to have tended more in the opposite direction—that of suppressing the desire to correct social injustices but supporting the desire to serve the country. When these findings are considered together with those of Table 3.8 (where we found that education consistently supported liberalism and non-hereditarianism, while residence suppressed them), one can reasonably conclude that familiarity with cosmopolitan issues, as represented by high educational attainment, made Black officials, as well as their White counterparts, more responsive to the needs of the disadvantaged. Perhaps it led them to draw more social distinctions within the nation as a whole in that respect, but surely it caused them to attribute invidious social differences to custom rather than to chromosome and made them feel government should be responsible for the well-being of its individual citizens. Familiarity with local issues, as represented by long-time residence in the same location, seems to have had just the opposite effects.

The associations between memberships and motivations do not reveal a very clear or consistent pattern, but a few observations may be made. In the South, the more Black officials desired to serve the country and the more they desired personal prestige and income, the fewer organizations they belonged to. Among southern White officials, however, these relationships were reversed: The desire to serve the country and to acquire personal prestige and income were positively (though still mildly) related to joining many organizations. Moreover, Black officials who desired to correct social injustices tended to join more organizations than did those who did not report such a desire, while their White counterparts revealed the opposite tendency. It is as though Black and White officials in the South saw their memberships in voluntary associations as serving quite different sets of objectives. Perhaps southern Black respondents viewed their organization memberships as particularized connections with groups having differentiated needs and powers, while southern White respondents may have viewed their memberships as generalized connections with an undifferentiated "public" or "citizenry." We return to this finding in Chapter 5.

Social Setting

Tables 3.10, 3.11, 3.12, 3.13, and 3.14 present the marginal distributions on population size, percent Black, party affiliation, region, and type of office. These tables are presented not only for the reader's general information, but also as further documentation of the *prima facie* representativeness of our sample of Black officials and of the correspondence of our White sample to the Black. Thus, note that the two samples are reassuringly similar with respect to the population size of the areas from which they were elected, their region, and their type of office. In Table 3.11 it is altogether expected, but still noteworthy, that some 45 percent of Black officials came from areas that were at least 50 percent Black, whereas only 13 percent of White officials came from such areas. Note also that Table 3.12 indicates that proportionately fewer of both samples were Republicans than Democrats with the difference being especially sharp among Black officials.

Table 3.15 presents the distributions of population size, percent Black, and party affiliation within each region. Note that population size and percent Black are here (and in all subsequent tables) standardized for

Table 3.10. Population Size of Election District (Percent)

Population Size	Black Officials	White Officials
Under 500	4	3
501–2,500	10	9
2,501–25,000	32	42
25,001–50,000	12	12
50,001–100,000	12	12
100,001–200,000	9	8
200,001–500,000	10	5
500,001–1,000,000	4	4
Over 1,000,000	6	5
Total	100 (732)	100 (479)

Table 3.11. Percent Black of Election District Population (Percent)

Percent Black	Black Officials	White Officials
0	1	14
1–9	10	30
10–19	12	13
20–29	11	12
30–39	12	8
40–49	9	10
50–59	8	6
60–69	8	3
70–79	7	2
80–89	8	2
90–99	11	—
100	4	—
Total	100 (747)	100 (469)

Table 3.12. Party Affiliation[a]

	Black Officials	White Officials
Democrat	77	58
Republican	13	34
Other	10	8
Total	100 (797)	100 (483)

[a] We were not able to find 1971 estimates of the distribution of Black officials by party affiliation within the universe of such officials. However, according to the National Republican Committee, 110 Black Republicans held elective office in 1970 (private communication). When this number is compared to the total number of Black elected officials (1,469) identified by the Joint Center for Political Studies in February 1970 (see Table 1.1), it would appear that about 7.5 percent of all Black elected officials in 1970 were Republicans.

Table 3.12. Region[a]

	Black Officials	White Officials
South	44	46
North	56	54
Total	100 (783)	100 (481)

[a] See Table 1.1 for breakdown by states.

Table 3.14. Type of Office[a]

Office	Black Officials	White Officials
State	11	18
County	10	5
City	43	37
Law	13	11
Education	24	30
Total	100 (799)	100 (484)

[a] See Table 1.2 for more detailed breakdown.

type of office as well as for race. This means, for example, that when we say an official represented an election area of "large" population we mean it was large relative to the populations of areas represented by others of his or her race who held the same type of office (state, county, city, law, or education). Such election areas were apt to be the more urban areas, whereas election areas of small population size were very likely to be the more rural areas, and we shall frequently refer to them as such. Similarly, when we say an official represented an election area having a "high" percent Black, we mean it was high relative to the percents Black of areas represented by those of his race who held the same type of office. This latter control is important to our analysis, because it takes into account the fact that state and city level offices, for example, within the same state necessarily differed in the absolute size of populations represented and almost certainly differed in the proportions of their represented populations that were Black. Standardization by type of office makes our population size and percent Black variables roughly comparable across all respondents of the same race, regardless of type of office.[3]

In Table 3.15 we see that more officials outside than inside the South came from areas of large population size, whereas more officials inside than outside the South came from areas of high percent Black population. And not unexpectedly, being a southern official increased one's chances of being a Democrat, but being a northern official increased one's chances of being a Republican.

Table 3.15. Social Setting Variables, by Race and Region[a]

Social Setting	Black Officials		White Officials	
	South	North	South	North
Large population size	27 (306)	54 (404)	33 (217)	47 (256)
High percent Black	64 (337)	45 (431)	78 (206)	41 (207)
Party affiliation				
Democrat	81	74	70	46
Republican	5	20	22	46
Other	14	7	9	8
Total	100 (339)	100 (435)	100 (220)	100 (256)
Type of office[b]				

[a] The first cell indicates that 27 percent of southern Black officials represented election districts of large population size.

[b] See Table 1.2.

Social Setting and Personal Background

Now let us see how these political setting variables related to the personal background variables discussed earlier. Table 3.16 presents the data on demographic settings, and Table 3.17, those on political settings.

Population Size. Inside the South, among both Black and White comparison officials, education bore a positive relation, and residence bore a negative relation to population size (although the strength of both associations was less among White than Black officials). Thus the more urban election areas of the South were likely to be represented by better-edu-

---

[3] See Appendix C.

Table 3.16. Associations Between Personal Background Variables and Demographic Setting Variables (Yule's Q)

	South				North			
	Residence	Education	Age	Memberships	Residence	Education	Age	Memberships
Black Officials								
Population size	−.32	.47	−.20	.58	.18	.40	.04	.31
Percent Black	.25	.28	.08	−.42	−.14	−.04	−.04	.26
White Officials								
Population size	−.02	.34	−.22	.64	.44	.24	.27	.26
Percent Black	.18	−.11	.08	−.30	−.02	−.02	.21	−.04

cated, more cosmopolitan officials and by officials who were newer residents in their communities. But in the North, residence as well as education carried a positive relation to population size. Metropolitan areas outside the South were thus apt to be represented by officials who were better-educated and also by officials who were longer-time residents.

Note also that among southern officials of both races the younger ones tended to represent the more urban areas, but outside the South there seems to have been no age difference. As one might expect, membership retained a positive association with population size across all respondent categories, probably indicating only the simple fact that where more voluntary associations are available, the rate of membership in them is apt to be higher.

Percent Black. In regard to the associations between personal background variables and percent Black of election area, we find that the relationships of percent Black to memberships was negative among southern Black officials but positive among their northern counterparts, while the relationship of percent Black to residence (and also education) was positive among the former but negative among the latter. This suggests that in southern high percent Black areas where, relative to low percent Black areas, Black officials tended to have higher local status (and also higher cosmopolitan status), they did not "need" the public certification of experience with social issues that memberships represent. In the North, Black officials in similar areas may have "needed" such certification more because they tended to have lower local (and also lower cosmopolitan) status. We discuss the possible electoral roles of memberships in general in Chapter 5.

Party Affiliation. Turning to Table 3.17, we find several interesting contrasts. First, among Black officials the residence and age levels of all three sets of party affiliates were higher, and their education levels were lower, inside than outside the South, thus indicating that the directions of regional tendencies shown in Table 3.5 were shared by all party affiliates. But note that the intensity of these regional differences varied from one party to the next, with the result that southern Black Republicans and northern Blacks who were affiliated with neither major party (i.e., "Other") held the most extreme positions with respect to residence, age, and education levels. Among White officials, although the same overall regional differences held, southern White Republican officials seem to have been markedly younger and more recent residents than were their Black counterparts. We have already seen earlier in this chapter that these party and racial differences in personal background were paralleled by strong differences in ideology, such that the older, earlier resident, and

Table 3.17. Personal Background Variables, by Political Setting Variables (Percent)[a]

	South				North			
	Residence	Education	Memberships	Age	Residence	Education	Memberships	Age
Black Officials								
Party Affiliation								
Democrat	59	48	46	46	39	51	43	45
Republican	75	31	47	75	44	56	60	49
Other	69	41	42	43	34	56	38	41
Type of Office								
State	59	74	72	29	39	49	51	49
County	77	24	48	54	44	44	42	39
City	58	42	43	48	42	39	47	43
Law	76	43	30	44	61	80	61	71
Education	54	54	46	50	26	55	37	37
White Officials								
Party Affiliation								
Democrat	56	31	32	49	45	52	44	36
Republican	29	36	38	40	48	43	41	42
Other	56	20	32	32	25	41	39	25
Type of Office								
State	40	57	57	31	56	54	52	33
County	69	*	17	54	*	*	*	*
City	44	26	36	48	44	44	43	36
Law	78	35	25	44	80	71	79	68
Education	48	25	17	51	31	42	26	34

[a] Among Black officials here, the smallest percentage base is 13; the largest is 316. Among White officials here, the smallest percentage base is 13; the largest is 148. The first cell indicates that 59 percent of southern Black officials who were affiliated with the Democratic party were long-time residents.

* Base less than 10; too small for percentaging.

less well-educated southern Black Republicans were very strongly integrationist, conservative, and preferred conventional-action, while the northern Black "Other" affiliates were strongly in favor of Black independence, liberalism, and direct-action.

Type of Office. Before examining our data on relationships between type of office and personal background, let us indicate the conceptual distinctions that we draw between state, county, and city government officials, on the one hand, and education and law officials on the other, and within each of these two groups of officials. The first group is thought of as functioning at different legislative-executive levels and the second as functioning in different kinds of social control agencies. In other words, the government officials listed at state, county, and city levels are primarily responsible for formulating and promulgating laws, directives, and other formal norms (always, of course, within boundaries set by higher levels—state, in the cases of county and city officials, and federal, in all cases), whereas persons holding office in education and law agencies are primarily responsible for inculcating and enforcing, respectively, these (as well as other) norms.

Among legislators-executives, we distinguish three levels (state, county, and city) in order to recognize differences in the scope of their jurisdictions, and among social control officials we distinguish between education and law as different kinds of social control. The jurisdictional scope distinction appears self-evident, but the distinction between kinds of social control deserves brief comment. Ideally, education agencies exert their influence over social behavior before infractions occur, and their social control function may therefore be called preventive. Law enforcement agencies, however, exert their most powerful influence after infractions have occurred, and their emphasis may therefore be called curative, segregative, and punitive.

Against this background, note the finding of Table 3.17 that in the South, among Black officials (and to a large extent, White officials as well), higher educational attainment, more memberships, younger age, and more recent residence were associated with holding legislative-executive office at the state level, in contrast with holding such office at the city, and particularly the county, level. Given these simple contrasts, plus the fact that liberalism, in particular, was positively associated with education and negatively associated with residence among all our respondents (Table 3.7), we should not be surprised to find later in this chapter that state officials tended to be quite strongly liberal, while county and city officials tended toward conservatism (Table 3.22). Outside the South, high educational attainment continued to be less associated with holding county and city office than with holding state office, although the relationship between them was considerably reduced. But note that in each race-by-region group county officials show the highest residence level, while state officials show the highest education level. Thus it seems fair to conclude that state officials and county officials were polar types in many respects, with city officials occupying an in-between position that linked them more closely to county than to state officials.

Similar contrasts may be observed among the two kinds of social control officials: Southern Black law enforcement officials had higher residence and lower education levels (also lower membership levels) than did education officials. Thus it would appear that in the South, a high degree of local experience was more of a qualification for Blacks holding county and city office and law enforcement office, while high cosmopolitan experience was more of a qualification for holding state office and education office.

A curious regional contrast emerges when we note, first, that Black officials (and also their White counterparts) holding state office showed much higher educational attainments inside than outside the South. But second, law enforcement officials (including magistrates and judges) of both races outside the South showed sharply higher educational attainments than inside the South. One might speculate that Black lawyers entering politics in the South gravitated more to the state level of legislative-executive office (or were blocked from election to law enforcement office), while those entering politics outside the South gravitated more to law enforcement office (or were blocked from election to legislative-executive office). We must emphasize that this is only a guess; our data provide no way of checking this possibility.

It therefore appears that outside the South punitive-curative social control (law enforcement) officials of both races were noticeably more highly educated and also more highly integrated into their communities by virtue of their more numerous voluntary association memberships as well as their older residencies than were preventive social control (education) officials. Inside the South, although law enforcement officials of both races had older residencies than education officials, the direction of all other relationships to personal background variables was reversed among Black officials and there were racial differences with respect to level of educational attainment and membership rate.[4]

---

[4] Some of these differences seem attributable to the fact that a much higher percentage of Black law officials in the North were judges and magistrates (and therefore highly educated) than in the South, while the reverse was true for justices of the peace and others (see Table 1.2)—a fact that was faithfully reflected in our Black (and also, therefore, our White) sample (see Table 1.3).

Social Setting and Attitudes

Demographic Setting. Our data also yield relationships between the attitude variables dealt with in the preceding chapter and the social setting variables. Table 3.18 presents the data relating the four ideology indexes, on the one hand, to population size and, on the other, to percent Black of the area from which the official was elected. Here we find that, among Black officials of both regions (and also, though less consistently, among their White counterparts), liberalism was positively related to region (southerners were more conservative), to urban areas (rural representatives were more conservative), and to percent Black (representatives of less heavily Black areas were more conservative). Preferences for Black independence and for direct-action were consistently more widespread among representatives of more heavily Black areas than of the less heavily Black areas.

Table 3.18. Ideologies, by Population Size and Percent Black (Percent)[a]

	South				North			
	Population Size				Population Size			
	Small		Large		Small		Large	
	Percent Black				Percent Black			
Ideologies	Low	High	Low	High	Low	High	Low	High
				Black Officials				
Hereditarianism	44	44	28	36	35	43	32	34
Direct-Action	44	54	52	58	53	57	51	57
Independence	46	66	52	61	46	61	40	56
Liberalism	27	27	43	47	33	45	63	68
				White Officials				
Hereditarianism	50	50	42	43	46	34	38	32
Liberalism	54	45	53	58	66	66	68	75

a Among Black officials here, the smallest percentage base is 28; the largest is 152. Among White officials here, the smallest percentage base is 19; the largest is 107. The first cell indicates that 44 percent of southern Black officials who represented election districts of small population size and low percent Black were hereditarian.

The relationship of hereditarianism to percent Black presents a puzzle: Outside the South, White officials show an overall negative association between percent Black and hereditarianism (−.19), while Black officials there show an overall positive association (.34). Table 3.18 shows this contrast held in urban as well as rural areas. The first finding is understandable on the basis of what seems a safe assumption that White officials who depend on proportionately more Black votes will (at least

because of political expediency) espouse less White supremacy hereditarianism than will those who depend on proportionately fewer Black
votes. But this argument should also hold for Black officials, and we should
therefore expect to find a negative hereditarianism-to-percent Black association among them as well. We do not find this; instead, outside the
South we find a positive relationship which can be explained by interpreting these Black officials' hereditarianism as often incorporating assertions of *Black* supremacy (or, perhaps, merely *difference*). We have no
evidence in our survey data by which this possibility can be tested, but one
comment in our interviews (from a northern official) seems to illustrate it.

> Why should we try some untried method? You know, if it worked
> for you, why not for us? And to that degree we should use what they
> call racism. During World War II, we were at war with both Ger-
> many and Japan, and yet the Germans were not arrested and put in
> concentration camps, but the Japanese were. So the whole spectrum
> of the country has been a racist-oriented thing from its inception.
> And if we are to play racism, then I say why not get in the game?
> Why stand on the outside? I am not a candidate for being poor and
> pure. I am a candidate for being a first-class citizen.

When we assume the presence of Black supremacy hereditarianism,
especially outside the South, a relatively simple symmetry of findings
in Table 3.18 among both Black respondents and White respondents
emerges: When they were hereditarian, officials of both races may have
tended to espouse own-race supremacy if they represented an election area
of high own-race population proportion, or more likely, the voters in these
areas may have favored the election of such officials.

Table 3.19 illuminates the relationships of motivations to the demographic variables. The most interesting findings here focus on the
desire to correct social injustices. Among Black officials, this desire was
stronger in the South than in the North, positively related to urbanization,
and positively related to percent Black. None of these relationships was
strong, but they were consistent.

Among the White counterparts of these officials, however, we find
that the desire to correct social injustices seems to have borne no clear
relationship to region, a slightly negative relationship to urbanization outside the South and mixed but strong relationships to urbanization inside
the South, and equally mixed and strong relationships to percent Black
inside the South. Consider the finding, for example, that in the more rural
areas of the South, White respondents' desire to correct social injustices
was inversely related to the percent Black of their election areas (Q =
.39), while in the more urban areas of this region, the relationship was

Table 3.19. Motivations, by Population Size and Percent Black (Percent)[a]

	South Population Size				North Population Size			
	Small		Large		Small		Large	
	Percent Black				Percent Black			
Motivations	Low	High	Low	High	Low	High	Low	High
	Black Officials							
Inside	80	52	72	71	65	55	56	63
Correct	78	79	85	87	67	80	78	85
Prestige	14	14	12	27	24	28	30	38
Serve	47	73	40	39	46	54	38	33
	White Officials							
Inside	26	39	38	42	43	33	36	38
Correct	47	28	6	40	35	36	33	30
Prestige	28	33	44	39	33	23	28	27
Serve	46	74	95	65	57	62	64	68

[a] Among Black officials here, the smallest percentage base is 22; the largest is 143. Among White officials here, the smallest percentage base is 16; the largest is 96. The first cell indicates that 80 percent of southern Black officials who represented election districts of small population size and low percent Black gave strong emphasis to being "on the inside."

strongly positive ($Q = .83$). Perhaps most striking of all is the finding that a mere 6 percent of White officials in southern urban areas of low percent Black gave first rank to the desire to correct social injustices. We return to this finding in Chapter 5.

Political Setting. Tables 3.20 and 3.21 reflect relationships between party affiliation and attitudes. Note that the widely advertised liberal-conservative distinctions between Democrats and Republicans of the same region, and between northerners and southerners of the same party, are manifested here—including the greater liberalism of southern White Republicans than of southern White Democrats. In fact, we have the curious phenomenon, with respect to the liberalism-conservatism difference, of White northern Democrats being more like White southern Republicans than White southern Democrats, and the latter being more like White northern Republicans than like White northern Democrats. No such ideological reversals appear among Black Democrats and Republicans; in both regions, Black Democrats were more liberal than Black Republicans.

It seems clear that the central ideological difference between Democrats and Republicans focused on liberalism versus conservatism, even when their respective positions were reversed. But the "Others" seem to

Table 3.20. Ideologies, by Party Affiliation (Percent)[a]

Ideologies	South Party Democrat	Republican	Other	North Party Democrat	Republican	Other
			Black Officials			
Hereditarianism	41	47	44	36	36	34
Direct-Action	50	38	62	60	31	76
Independence	58	19	76	52	38	69
Liberalism	32	12	30	56	44	59
			White Officials			
Hereditarianism	45	46	63	35	41	30
Liberalism	48	62	39	78	58	60

[a] Among Black officials here, the smallest percentage base is 15; the largest is 314. Among White officials here, the smallest percentage base is 18; the largest is 143. The first cell indicates that 41 percent of southern Black officials who were affiliated with the Democratic party were hereditarian.

have been distinguished from affiliates of both these established parties by other issues. Among the Blacks in both regions the distinction centered on the preferences for Black independence and direct-action (i.e., "militancy," as that term was discussed earlier) of the "Others" versus the greater integrationism and conventional-action of the Republicans and Democrats. Among the Whites in the South, at least, the central distinction was probably the White-supremacist hereditarianism of the "Others" versus the greater non-hereditarianism of the Democrats and Republicans. Unfortunately, our data give no indication of what the distinguishing ideological feature of northern White "Other" affiliates may have been; the ideological differences shown in Table 3.20 between the Republicans and Democrats, on the one hand, and "Others," on the other, seem too mild.

Turning to Table 3.21, we find that, among Black officials, Republicans in 1971 were more likely to want to be "on the inside" and less likely to be motivated by the other desires shown. Democrats and "Other" affiliates were more inclined to want to correct social injustices and also slightly more inclined to want to serve the country. The data on the prestige motive among Black officials are less regular, as are the data on White officials.

The relationships of type of office to ideologies and motivations are shown in Tables 3.22 and 3.23. Among the three types of legislative-executive office, southern state officials (both Black and White) were more liberal, less hereditarian, and more favorable toward direct-action than officials at other levels. Except for direct-action, the same relationships held outside the South, as well. It is interesting to note that southern Black

Table 3.21. Motivations, by Party Affiliation (Percent)[a]

Motivations	South Party			North Party		
	Democrat	Republican	Other	Democrat	Republican	Other
			Black Officials			
Inside	62	73	61	59	63	61
Correct	80	75	83	80	70	82
Prestige	17	*	14	33	27	18
Serve	58	58	62	43	38	40
			White Officials			
Inside	40	44	13	41	38	50
Correct	34	25	20	46	23	16
Prestige	31	44	33	30	25	39
Serve	73	70	72	52	70	74

[a] Among Black officials here, the smallest percentage base is 11; the largest is 295. Among White officials here, the smallest percentage base is 15; the largest is 137. The first cell indicates that 62 percent of southern Black officials who were affiliated with the Democratic party gave strong emphasis to being "on the inside."

* Base less than 10; too small for percentaging.

county officials, for whom Table 3.17 has shown markedly longer-time residencies and markedly lower educational attainments, were also more strongly inclined toward Black independence and more hereditarian than southern state or city officials. Outside the South, these contrasts were blurred, but still present in broad outlines.

Among the social control offices, we find a series of striking contrasts, beginning with the fact that northern Black law officials were far less hereditarian than any other group of Black or White officials shown. Northern Black law officials were also clearly more integrationist, more liberal, and more conventional-actionist than were their southern counterparts. Since it will be remembered from Table 3.17 that the former were also much better educated, older, belonged to more voluntary associations, and were more recent residents, it seems clear that some of the differences between Black law officials in the two regions were the result of selection-before-office rather than experience-in-office.

Other contrasts emerge when we examine education officials: Inside the South, they were less hereditarian than law officials, but outside the South they were clearly more favorably inclined toward independence as well as more hereditarian. Again, Table 3.17 has shown that at least some of these differences were attributable to selection: Inside the South, the levels of educational attainment, age, and memberships of education officials were all higher than those of law officials, but outside the South the

Table 3.22. Ideologies, by Type of Office (Percent)ᵃ

Ideologies	South Office					North Office				
	State	County	City	Law	Education	State	County	City	Law	Education
Black Officials										
Hereditarianism	36	46	38	58	41	34	42	45	19	31
Direct-Action	59	54	47	63	51	56	66	52	46	60
Independence	59	73	53	66	62	47	54	54	26	57
Liberalism	62	24	26	29	30	68	46	46	60	56
White Officials										
Hereditarianism	32	46	48	44	58	28	*	40	40	38
Liberalism	77	38	46	52	40	72	*	66	83	63

ᵃAmong Black officials here, the smallest percentage base is 31; the largest is 165. Among White officials here, the smallest percentage base is 11; the largest is 97. The first cell indicates that 36 percent of southern Black officials who held state office were hereditarian.

* Base less than 10; too small for percentaging.

Table 3.23. Motivations, by Type of Office (Percent)[a]

Motivations	South					North				
	State	County	Office City	Law	Education	State	County	Office City	Law	Education
					Black Officials					
Inside	76	50	62	50	69	67	53	60	45	66
Correct	90	83	76	87	86	76	70	81	57	85
Prestige	28	14	12	33	14	24	31	23	76	20
Serve	32	65	61	73	55	33	46	49	30	40
					White Officials					
Inside	31	*	41	26	44	31	*	41	41	45
Correct	61	*	16	38	25	58	*	34	30	24
Prestige	41	*	36	44	19	36	*	29	56	21
Serve	52	60	83	68	71	48	*	63	61	66

[a] Among Black officials here, the smallest percentage base is 21; the largest is 155. Among White officials here, the smallest percentage base is 10; the largest is 95. The first cell indicates that 76 percent of southern Black officials who held state office gave strong emphasis to being "on the inside."

* Base less than 10; too small for percentaging.

reverse was true. These reversals seem to have been due mainly to higher levels on each variable among law officials outside than inside the South, but partly to lower levels among education officials.

Certain of these contrasts carry over to Table 3.23. For example, the greater liberalism of state officials was paralleled (with one minor exception among northern Black officials) by their greater concern with correcting social injustices and lesser concern with serving the country.

We also note that the two types of social control officials were again in contrast, chiefly because law enforcement officials more strongly adopted personal prestige as their motivation for seeking office but rejected being "on the inside," while education officials just as strongly rejected personal prestige and desired to be "on the inside." It may be that law enforcement officials of both races and both regions felt that public prestige lay more within their grasp (perhaps because of the prestige accorded to the legal profession, and perhaps also because of their greater ability to "make headlines") than did being "on the inside" of things (where legislative and executive decisions are made, rather than enforced). Education officials, on the other hand, may have felt that insider status was a realistic goal for them because their offices are not restricted to administering policy that is made by others; they frequently make such policy themselves. At the same time, the public controversies that so often rage around those policies may have been thought by education officials to deny them prestige.

Note also that southern Black law officials differed sharply from their northern counterparts in having greater desire to correct social injustices, less desire for personal prestige and income, and greater desire to serve the country. This latter finding poses a problem of interpretation (especially in view of the fact that southern law officials' level of concern with serving the country was the highest of all categories of Blacks shown). Some of this seems attributable to a pervasive regional difference in attitude; southern officials of both races were generally more likely to say they sought governmental office because of a desire to serve the country than were northern officials. But in addition, it is conceivable that southern Black law officials may have identified their "country" more with its ideal law—the Constitution of the United States—than with its real institutions, which they clearly wanted to change as much as did any other group of Black officials and more than their northern counterparts.

CHAPTER 4 □□
Sex Differences

An individual's gender is similar to his or her race, insofar as both are social identifications based on physiological characteristics and both have been culturally assigned a wide range of implications. However, while race identification is a variable with which this study is concerned in every phase of its analysis, we can examine sex identification in a special chapter only, because so few women (89 Black and 34 White) were included in our sample. Moreover, because our sample contains only nine White women in the southern region, we were forced to omit the South versus North regional control in the following analysis.

Personal Background

The first question we asked of our data was whether officials' sex identifications were related to the other personal background characteristics examined in this study. And, as Table 4.1 indicates, we found stronger associations between sex and all four personal background variables among White officials than among Black officials. Thus male White officials reported longer residencies, more total voluntary association memberships, greater age, and higher education than did female White officials. Although the direction of these relationships remains the same among Black officials, their strength is considerably reduced. It should also be noted that Black officials were higher on all the personal background variables than were their same-sex White counterparts and that

Table 4.1. Personal Background Variables, by Sex (Percent)[a]

| | Black Officials | | White Officials | |
	Male	Female	Male	Female
Longer residence	50	45	48	29
Higher education	51	40	41	30
Older age	46	46	42	34
More memberships	46	42	39	29

[a] Among Black officials here, the smallest percentage base is 65; the largest is 671. Among White officials here, the smallest percentage base is 27; the largest is 437. The first cell indicates that 50 percent of male Black officials were long-time residents.

these race-related differences were slightly more pronounced among women than men.

Social Setting

In Table 4.2, we show the associations between sex identification and social setting variables. Note that in both samples of officials (especially White) males tended to represent the more populous election areas, and females the less populous. A further similarity between the Black and White samples is found with respect to the relationship between sex and racial composition of the area represented. Thus among Black officials the higher the percent Black of election district, the more likely was the official to be female, and since the association between maleness and percent *non-Black* among White comparison officials was also negative (reversing the sign of association between maleness and percent Black), we may conclude that the more race-homogeneous areas tended to be represented by females (of their own race), while the more race-heterogeneous areas tended to be represented by males (also of their own race).[1]

However, Table 4.3 (despite a frequently decimated case base) indicates the possibility that these findings, so similar between the two races, may actually be explained by somewhat different factors in each. Among our White respondents, the predominance of White women as officials in the high percent White (low percent Black) areas may be largely accounted for by their greater overrepresentation in only one type of office (education) and especially by White males' severe underrepresentation in

---

[1] We should add our belief that these findings are not direct artifacts of the way the White sample was selected, although they could conceivably be indirect ones. As indicated in Chapter 1, we systematically matched White officials with Black officials on the explicit basis of type of office and geographical location. But neither the sexual identification of official, nor the racial composition of his or her election area, was an explicit criterion of matching.

Table 4.2. Social Setting Variables, by Sex (Percent)

	Black Officials		White Officials	
	Males	Females	Males	Females
Large population size	43 (636)	38 (69)	42 (440)	28 (32)
High percent Black	52 (683)	74 (87)	60 (384)	48 (27)
Party				
Democrat	77	81	57	53
Republican	13	9	34	41
Other	10	10	8	6
Total	100 (687)	100 (88)	100 (441)	100 (34)
Type of office				
State	11	14	18	9
County	10	14	4	3
City	44	29	38	15
Law	13	6	12	6
Education	22	38	28	68
Total	100 (686)	100 (87)	100 (443)	100 (34)
Southern region	42 (692)	41 (89)	47 (446)	28 (34)

Table 4.3. Type of Office, by Sex, Population Size, and Percent Black (Percent)

	Population Size							
	Small				Large			
	Percent Black				Percent Black			
Type of	Low		High		Low		High	
office	Male	Female	Male	Female	Male	Female	Male	Female
	Black Officials							
State	12	*	10	11	12	7	14	8
County	10	*	9	17	11	7	8	—
City	50	*	49	43	41	29	33	25
Law	9	*	13	3	14	14	13	8
Education	19	*	19	26	22	43	31	58
Total	100 (139)	(8)	100 (225)	100 (35)	100 (187)	100 (14)	100 (84)	100 (12)
	White Officials							
State	21	—	10	*	22	*	29	*
County	3	—	4	*	7	*	5	*
City	34	20	43	*	43	*	29	*
Law	11	—	14	*	20	*	9	*
Education	31	80	29	*	8	*	27	*
Total	100 (71)	100 (10)	100 (136)	(7)	100 (82)	(3)	100 (92)	(5)

* Base less than 10, too small for percentaging.

education offices in areas of large population and high percent White. Among Black respondents, the distribution of women among types of offices appears to have been less restricted, so that their predominance in areas of high percent Black may have been due to greater representation in state, county, and city levels of office, as well as education offices.

Returning to Table 4.2, we find indications that a slightly larger percentage of Black female than male officials were Democrats, while slightly more Black male than female officials were Republicans. The reverse seems to have been the case among White officials. Table 4.4 elaborates on these findings only in the most speculative manner, because it repeatedly exhausts our case base. Once this is recognized, however, the table suggests the possibility that Black female officials were indeed more likely than Black male officials to be Democrats in every type of election area *except* the heavily populated ones of low percent Black and that Black male officials were more likely than Black female officials to be Republicans and also more likely to be "Other" in all types of areas.

Table 4.4. Party Affiliation, by Sex, Population Size, and Percent Black of Election Area (Percent)

				Population Size				
			Small				Large	
				Percent Black				
	Low		High		Low		High	
Party	Male	Female	Male	Female	Male	Female	Male	Female
				Black Officials				
Democrat	74	*	79	89	73	71	82	92
Republican	16	*	7	3	19	21	12	8
Other	9	*	14	9	8	7	6	—
Total	100 (139)	(8)	100 (223)	100 (35)	100 (186)	100 (14)	100 (84)	100 (12)
				White Officials				
Democrat	41	60	67	*	53	*	60	*
Republican	49	30	22	*	41	*	33	*
Other	10	10	10	*	6	*	8	*
Total	100 (71)	100 (10)	100 (135)	(7)	100 (81)	(3)	100 (92)	(5)

* Base less than 10, too small for percentaging.

With regard to the bearing of sex on type of office, Table 4.2 indicates that among both races men predominated at the city level of governmental office and among law agency offices, while women predominated among education agency offices. Table 4.3 bears out these findings (with one minor exception) across all categories of population size and percent Black, but adds that among officials of both races the predominance of men at the city level of office was less in areas of high percent own-race population. This table also indicates that among the remaining two types of legislative-executive officials (state and county) Black women seem to have predominated over Black men in the less populous areas, but the reverse was true in the more populous ones. The predominance of White men over White women in these types of office seems more consistent.

Attitudes

With respect to the bearing of sex on the attitudes discussed in Chapters 2 and 3, Table 4.5 indicates that the Black women in our sample were more favorably inclined toward Black independence than were Black men, and White women were more liberal than White men. Women of each race were more oriented toward correcting social injustices and were less hereditarian than men of the same race. And again we find that sex differences were generally greater among White officials than among Black.

Table 4.5. Attitude Variables, by Sex (Percent)[a]

	Black Officials		White Officials	
	Males	Females	Males	Females
Ideologies				
Hereditarianism	39	32	43	27
Direct-Action	53	52		
Independence	53	66		
Liberalism	44	39	58	68
Motivations				
Inside	38	40	39	52
Correct	78	88	31	43
Prestige	25	23	32	18
Serve	49	48	67	62

[a]Among Black officials here, the smallest percentage base is 57; the largest is 682. Among White officials here, the smallest percentage base is 27; the largest is 439. The first cell indicates that 39 percent of male Black officials were hereditarian.

Because of their special *prima facie* relevance to sex identification and to social relations between the sexes, we now introduce three attitude variables that have not been examined in earlier chapters.

Sex-Related Attitude Variables

The first of these we call "birth control," and it is based on Black respondents' answers to the following question: "In your opinion, how important [is birth control] in achieving real progress for Blacks in America? Very Important; Fairly Important; Not too Important; Not Important at All." In the analysis that follows, "Very Important" and "Fairly Important" replies are grouped together as "High" importance.

The second sex-related attitude variable is called "care centers" and represents Black respondents' answers to the following question: "In your opinion, how important [are free health and day-care centers] in achieving real progress for Blacks in America? Very Important; Fairly Important; Not too Important; Not Important at All." In the analysis that follows, "Very Important" and "Fairly Important" replies are grouped together as "High" importance.

The third sex-related attitude variable is called "women's rights" and represents replies to the following question, asked of both Black and White respondents: "Women should have the same social, economic, and political rights as men, even if it involves taking some rights away from men. Strongly Agree; Agree; No Opinion; Disagree; Strongly Disagree." In the analysis that follows, "Strongly Agree" and "Agree" responses are grouped together as "High" importance.

Table 4.6 indicates that among Black officials of both sexes care centers were considerably more highly evaluated as instruments of Black progress than was birth control. Female Black officials were somewhat more in favor of birth control, and very slightly more in favor of care centers, than were male Black officials. With respect to their attitude towards women's rights, there was no difference between male and female Black officials, but female White officials were slightly more in favor of women's rights than were male White officials.

When we inquire about associations among the three sex-related attitude variables, Table 4.7 suggests several differences between male and female Black officials. Indeed, this table indicates that although men were just as likely to say they approved women's rights as were women

Table 4.6. Attitudes Toward Sex-Related Issues (Percent)[a]

	Black Officials		White Officials	
	Males	Females	Males	Females
Birth control[b]	38	48		
Care centers[b]	75	79		
Women's rights[c]	57	58	60	65

[a]Among Black officials here, the smallest percentage base is 80; the largest is 648. Among White officials here, the smallest percentage base is 34; the largest is 423. The first cell indicates that 38 percent of male Black officials favored birth control.

[b]Percent "Very Important" plus percent "Fairly Important."

[c]Percent "Strongly Agree" plus percent "Agree."

(Table 4.6), they held radically different ideas about the meaning of such approval. For women, it meant more stress on health and day-care centers; for men it did not. And for women, it meant more emphasis on birth control than it did for men. One relatively straightforward interpretation of these findings is that in the male mind women's rights may have been more of an abstraction, a principle to be believed in or not, while in the female mind these rights may have been a practical problem to be solved by concrete action or exacerbated by lack of it. But there is another, more complicated interpretation, wherein the Black men and women in our sample may have held different assessments regarding the compatibility of efforts to equalize the races and efforts to equalize the sexes.

Table 4.7. Associations among Attitudes Toward Sex-Related Issues (Yule's Q)

| | Male | | Female | |
	Care Centers	Women's Rights	Care Centers	Women's Rights
Birth control	.63	.17	.18	.29
Care centers		.05		.41

In order to describe this interpretation, we begin by noting that the birth control and care centers attitude data are based on questions asked with specific reference to "progress for Blacks in America," while women's rights attitude data are based on a question asked without specific reference. Thus respondents who may have supported birth control and care centers, say, for *women's* progress (or for some other reason) but rejected them for *Blacks'* progress, would logically have given negative responses to the question as phrased. As a consequence, the "progress for Blacks in America" restriction probably underestimates the level of overall, variously motivated support for birth control and care centers. But since there does not seem to be any reason to suspect that this underestimation varied systematically with the respondent's sex, it is not likely to affect comparisons on these questions between the sexes. However, there may be another effect worth noting. This involves the associations of the women's rights variable with the other two. In light of what we have said concerning the different phrasing of these questions, it seems likely that only those Black respondents who believed not only that birth control or care centers served Black progress but also that Black progress and women's progress were compatible social goals could respond positively to both the women's rights question and the birth control or care center question. This restriction almost certainly depressed the level of association between the women's rights data, on the one hand, and the birth control and care centers data, on the other, in proportion to the extent (unknown in this study) to which Black progress and women's progress were considered incompatible social goals.

As a result, it seems reasonable to think that part of the male-female difference in Black officials' associations between women's rights, on the one hand, and birth control and care centers, on the other, reflects different assessments of compatibility between Black progress and women's progress—such that female Black officials viewed these two social goals as more compatible than did male Black officials.

In this light, it does not seem surprising that Table 4.8 shows a greater tendency among female Black officials than among their male counterparts to connect positive orientations toward each of the sex-related issues with a positive orientation toward Black independence. That is, Black women simply did not see as much of a contradiction between what might be called racial radicalism and sexual radicalism as did Black men. It is as though Black males believed that one had to choose between being radical on matters of race or on matters of sex; Black females seem to have believed that such a choice was not so necessary. Perhaps this difference formed an important element in the contrast between the following two interview statements by a male official and a female, respectively.

I heard a female Black official saying that she's been discriminated against more because she's a woman than she has been for being Black. That bothers me, because I know women catch hell, but nobody catches hell like Black people.

*

Since I've been in the political arena, I have met more discrimination as a woman than being Black, because Black males are no different in this basic respect. Males in America have a certain feeling toward women in decision-making roles. It has nothing to do with color, but it's a little bit deeper with Blacks because of the fact that the so-called Black matriarchal society that developed in America as a result of what the American society did to the Black male gets in the way of Black men actually coming to recognize that they need the Black woman to supplement all of their efforts if they are eventually going to liberate our people.

Note, in Table 4.8, that the magnitude of association coefficients between birth control and care centers, on the one hand, and each ideology and motivation, on the other, was generally greater among women than among men. This accords with our earlier inference that birth control and care centers were more significant issues for women than for men inasmuch as it indicates that these issues were more closely integrated into the women's total belief systems, even though the women did not differ much from the men in the direction or strength of their attitudes toward each of these issues viewed separately (Table 4.6).

But now consider the relationships involving attitudes toward birth control and care centers among the women alone. Contrasting patterns are revealed in Table 4.8: Support for birth control as a means toward Black

Table 4.8. Associations Between Attitudes Toward Sex-Related Issues and Ideologies and Motivations, by Sex (Yule's Q)

| | Attitudes | | | | | | | |
| | Birth Control | | Care Centers | | Women's Rights | | | |
	Black Males	Black Females	Black Males	Black Females	Black Males	Black Females	White Males	White Females
Ideologies								
Hereditarianism	—.17	.42	.06	—.26	—.13	—.02	—.24	—.32
Direct-Action	—.11	—.02	—.16	—.26	.24	.30		
Independence	—.28	.11	.05	.32	—.11	.06		
Liberalism	.06	—.43	.09	.86	.37	.32	.43	.03
Motivations								
Inside	—.02	—.52	.00	.55	.13	.10	.03	.54
Correct	.11	—.25	.39	.54	.01	—.08	.28	.40
Prestige	.02	.11	—.18	.66	.03	.05	.05	.39
Serve	—.07	.55	.15	.38	—.24	—.03	—.25	—.67

progress was associated with hereditarianism, conservatism, and the absence of a desire to correct social injustices, while support for care centers was associated with non-hereditarianism, liberalism, and a desire to correct social injustices. Moreover, although support of birth control as well as care centers was associated with support for Black independence, the association of care centers was the stronger, and whereas support for each was associated with the desire to serve the country, the association of birth control was the stronger. Finally, the association of care centers with the desire to be "on the inside" (which we have shown was largely instrumental to correcting social injustices) was positive, while the association of this desire with birth control was negative.

The picture that emerges from all this reveals female Black officials' support for the birth control means toward Black progress as more linked to conservative and patriotically oriented (rather than liberal and reformist oriented) goals and motivations, and also more accepting of hereditarianism. Care centers support, however, seems to have carried just the opposite attitudinal linkages. Clearly, proposals to limit the number of Black people before birth and to care for Black people after birth meant quite different things ideologically to female Black officials.

Attitudes Toward Birth Control

Let us examine these different meanings by introducing an additional variable, namely, respondents' belief that "When people talk about birth control, they really mean birth control for Black people, not White people." Such a belief is here taken to indicate the extent to which birth control advocacy was thought to be racially discriminatory or, more to the point in this case, genocidal. In this general regard, consider the following comment from a male Black official:

I'm very much in favor of birth control but I'm very much opposed to birth control being imposed upon Black people and that's what seems to me to be the stance of several of the agencies involved in birth control. I was in a city some two years ago with a large Black and large Catholic population and one of the agencies was conducting an experiment in the distribution of birth control devices only in the Black community. Now here was the large White population with families of 5, 6, 8, 10 children and no attempt was being made to have them stop having babies. But a serious attempt was being made to convince Black women that they ought not to have additional children. That's nothing but racism and it's genocide really, trying to destroy a nation of people. So I'm in favor of birth control but I think that's an option that has to be left up to the mother whether she's White or Black. If a Black woman on welfare has six children and wants six more that's her option. If she wants birth control devices, she ought to have their availability, but she ought not have them imposed upon her.

The overall distributions of responses to whether birth control advocacy was racially discriminatory are summarized in Table 4.9, where the differences between Black and White officials are striking; 34 percent of Black officials agreed that racially discriminatory implications were present, while only 4 percent of their White counterparts agreed; 89 percent of the latter disagreed, while only 50 percent of the former disagreed. But in some contrast with these differences between the races, there was a notable similarity between officials of the same sex across race. Thus, the associations between sex and agreement[2] that birth control advocacy is discriminatory were nearly the same among Whites (.11) as among Blacks

---

[2] In order to distribute our cases evenly and retain comparability between percentage data on Black officials and White officials, we dichotomized responses between "No Opinion" and "Disagree." As a result, the homogeneous category is "Disagree"; the other category referred to here as "Agree" is residual and somewhat heterogeneous insofar as it contains "No Opinion" responses as well as "Agree" and "Strongly Agree" responses.

(.14). This means that both Black and White female officials were somewhat less inclined to agree than were their respective male counterparts. Although we have no data on this point, it seems likely that the sex relationship of birth control was more important to the women of both races than it was to the men. At least this accords with our earlier speculation that Black females were more likely than males to segregate their sex-related and race-related ideologies.

Table 4.9. "When people talk about birth control they really mean birth control for Black people, not White people." (Percent)

	Black Officials	White Officials
Strongly agree	12	1
Agree	22	3
No opinion	15	6
Disagree	42	53
Strongly disagree	8	36
Total	100 (772)	100 (476)

In seeking an understanding of the different connotations among Black officials of support for birth control and for care centers (as discussed earlier in connection with Table 4.8), consider that the association between agreement that birth control advocacy was discriminatory and support for birth control as an instrument of Black progress was strongly negative (—.51 among female Black officials and —.43 among male Black officials). As expected, then, the more one believed that birth control advocacy was discriminatory, the less one advocated birth control as a means toward Black progress. The situation was reversed, however, for care centers: The association between belief that birth control advocacy was discriminatory and support for care centers was .03 among female, and .24 among male Black officials. Thus the more one thought limitation of population before birth is tainted by anti-Black racism, the more one advocated care for the Black population after birth.

It is likely, then, that birth control per se might have received greater favor among Black officials had it not carried racist implications. In this connection it is also noteworthy that, although female Black officials registered a higher level of approval of birth control as a means toward Black progress than did male Black officials (Table 4.6), the women's approval was more strongly restrained by their belief in the discriminatory connotations of birth control advocacy (—.51) than was the men's approval (—.43). Therefore, if the discriminatory connotations were removed, the level of birth control approval among all Black officials would almost surely rise and more quickly among Black women than among Black men.

But in the meantime, this analysis makes it understandable that support of birth control as an instrument of Black progress was left largely to those Black officials whom Table 4.8 described as conservative, patriotic, and hereditarian, while care centers—because they did not connote discrimination against Black people—rallied support from liberals, reformists, and non-hereditarians.

Connotations of Birth Control Advocacy

Since the racial connotations of birth control advocacy have figured so prominently in the preceding analysis, it may be of interest to digress for a moment and examine some possible correlations of these connotations—specifically, officials' educational attainment and the demographic character of their election areas.

In examining the relationship of education to belief that birth control advocacy was discriminatory, we found a negative association among Black officials (—.28) but a slight positive one (.06) among White officials (data on both sexes were combined in both cases). It therefore appears that although more formal education decreased the likelihood that Black officials would think that birth control advocacy was discriminatory against Blacks, it did not have this effect on White officials.

Could this have been the same education in both cases? The relevant data we have bear only on whether an official's undergraduate college was predominantly Black or White. Since all but one White official had attended a predominantly White college and since more education for them entailed slightly more belief that birth control advocacy was discriminatory, we should expect attendance at similar colleges to have a similar impact on Black officials—if Blacks and Whites had had similar experiences at these colleges.

What we found, however, is that Black officials who, like their White counterparts, had attended predominantly White colleges were *less* believing that birth control advocacy was discriminatory than were Black officials who, unlike their White counterparts, had attended predominantly Black colleges (Q = —.29). Thus, with reference to the attribution of discrimination to advocacy of birth control, the contrast between Blacks and Whites who attended White colleges is greater than between Whites who attended White colleges and Blacks who attended Black colleges. It therefore seems likely that the experience of higher education was quite different for Blacks and Whites attending the same type of college.

We can press our data one step further in trying to understand this contrast. We have indicated that belief in the discriminatory connotations of birth control advocacy was negatively related to education among Black officials but not among White officials. We have also found that education was negatively related to hereditarianism among both Black and White respondents (Table 3.7). Now we may ask whether education had the same effect among Blacks and Whites on the belief that birth control advocacy was discriminatory, regardless of one's views on the social relevance of genetic differences between the races (and presumably, therefore, regardless of one's views on the social justice of racially discriminatory birth control). Table 4.10 addresses this question.

Table 4.10. Percent Believing that Birth Control Advocacy Is Discriminatory, by Hereditarianism, and Education[a]

| | Hereditarianism | | | |
| | No Education | | Yes Education | |
	Low	High	Low	High
All Black officials	55	35	57	57
All White officials	9	12	8	5

[a]Among Black officials here, the smallest percentage base is 72; the largest is 223. Among White officials, the smallest percentage base is 43; the largest is 120. The first cell indicates that 55 percent of all Black officials who were non-hereditarian and had low education believed that birth control advocacy is discriminatory.

The evidence here is that if a Black official was non-hereditarian, education made it less likely that he or she would believe birth control advocacy is discriminatory. White non-hereditarians, however, seem to have been impelled in the opposite direction; with more education, they became slightly more likely to believe that birth control advocacy is discriminatory. Education may have taught Black officials who believed the genetic inheritances of Blacks and Whites were not relevant to social relations between the races that birth control carried other, nondiscriminatory connotations. At the same time, education may have led White officials who also did not believe in the social relevance of genetic differences between Blacks and Whites to the view that, in addition to its other relevancies, birth control carried racially discriminatory ones as well.

As a result, it seems that education not only lowered the levels of hereditarianism among Black and White officials (Table 3.7), but also brought non-hereditarians of both races closer together in their appraisal of the racial significance of birth control. In this sense, our data suggest that the experience of higher education did indeed differ for Blacks and Whites, such that Whites became less hereditarian themselves, but more apt to perceive it in their White fellows and in White institutions, while Blacks became both less hereditarian and less inclined to perceive it in the birth control issue and birth control advocacy.

Demographic Setting

Let us examine now the relationships of population size and percent Black to agreement that birth control advocacy is discriminatory. The data are presented in Table 4.11. Agreement seems to have been positively related to percent Black, but negatively related to population size (urbanization), among male as well as female Black officials, meaning that where the Black population was more rural, and also where it was larger in proportion to the surrounding White population, Black elected officials were more likely to view birth control advocacy as racially discriminatory. Considering the overall positive associations among Black officials of education with urbanization and also with percent Black (Table 2.17), some of

Table 4.11. Associations Between Belief that Birth Control Advocacy Is Race-Focused, and Population Size and Percent Black, Holding Constant Sex (Yule's Q)

	Males	Females
	Black Officials	
Population size	—.28	—.14
Percent Black	.33	.14
	White Officials	
Population size	.33	—1.00
Percent Black	.06	.00

the rural concentration of that view is attributable to rural-urban differences in educational attainment. But its greater concentration in areas of high percent Black is, of course, not so readily attributable. One may speculate that Black officials defined birth control advocacy as a racist step designed to restrain or reduce voting strength of the larger Black communities and thus reduce the power and number of their elected representatives in government. Indeed, it may be said in interpreting all evidence of Black opposition to birth control that for a people long oppressed economically, politically, educationally, and otherwise, sheer population size can become a zealously defended resource of social power. This seems true even where representation in governmental institutions is not an issue and all the more so where it is.

Other Sex-Related Attitudes

Returning now to complete our examination of Table 4.8, we find some interesting contrasts between the attitudes of Black officials and their White counterparts toward women's rights. For example, among

White officials the relationship of women's rights to each of the indicated motivations for seeking public office was stronger among women than men, whereas no such consistent pattern emerges among Black officials. Following our earlier argument, this seems to suggest that women's rights was a more ideologically integrated, and in this sense significant, issue to female White officials than to their male White counterparts, but not clearly more significant to female Black officials than to male Black officials.

In summary, then, our data indicate that birth control and care centers (but not women's rights) were ideologically and motivationally more significant issues to female Black officials than to male Black officials and that women's rights were more significant to female White officials than to their male counterparts.

Before leaving Table 4.8, certain other relationships should be noted. For example, the associations between hereditarianism and support of women's rights are uniformly negative (but least so among Black female officials), thus suggesting the possibility that the less one believes inherited *racial* characteristics matter in life achievement, the less one is likely to believe inherited *sexual* characteristics matter in that achievement. We find also that the relationship between support of women's rights and liberalism is uniformly positive (but least so among White female officials), thus suggesting that the more one believes that rights should be equalized between women and men, the more one is likely also to believe that the federal government should be responsible for guaranteeing that equalization. However, it is worth noting that, among Black officials of both sexes, support of women's rights was positively (though moderately) associated with preference for direct-action. This suggests that although the federal government may have been viewed as a prime agent for equalizing rights between the sexes, mass public action may have been seen as a principal means for insuring that the government takes such action.

Attitudes and Personal Background

Table 4.12 summarizes the personal background correlates of the three sex-related attitudes on which this chapter centers. Notice again that the associations generally tend to be larger among women than men, indicating a more systematic, less random quality in women's attitudes. Beyond this general observation, however, we find that support for women's rights bore an expected consistently negative relationship to residence (our presumed indicator of local interests) and a consistently positive relationship to education (our presumed indicator of cosmopolitan interests). Note also that education was positively related (with one exception) to all three of the sex-related attitudes among female Black officials, including birth control (undoubtedly a result of the effect of education on the belief that birth control advocacy was discriminatory—see Table 4.10). And somewhat surprisingly, older officials were (again with one exception) slightly more favorably inclined toward each sex-related issue.

Table 4.12. Associations Between Attitudes Toward Sex-Related Issues and Personal Background Variables, by Sex (Yule's Q)

	Attitudes							
	Birth Control		Care Centers		Women's Rights			
	Black Males	Black Females	Black Males	Black Females	Black Males	Black Females	White Males	White Females
Residence	—.01	.26	.09	—.26	—.12	—.22	—.12	.64
Education	.15	.58	—.18	.26	.09	.09	—.09	.33
Age	.17	.10	.15	.11	.29	.44	—.30	.42
Memberships	—.12	.03	—.19	.03	.30	—.04	.10	.58

Attitudes and Social Setting

The social setting correlates of the three sex-related attitudes are shown in Tables 4.13, 4.14, and 4.15. Examining first the demographic variables, we find that there was more support for women's rights among northern officials of both races than among their southern counterparts, and although female southern Black officials showed more support for birth control as a means toward Black progress than did female northern Black officials, the reverse trend appeared among the males.

Further, the more populous (i.e., urban) the election area, the more elected officials of both sexes supported birth control and women's rights, and the more female Black officials supported care centers. Agreement with women's rights seems to have been an attitude more strongly associated with urbanization among female White officials and least strongly associated with it among male White officials.

And, in full accord with our tentative conclusion (set forth earlier in this chapter) that support for birth control, particularly in the high percent Black areas, was restrained by the belief that such advocacy was racially discriminatory, we find that the higher the percent Black, the less likely officials were to approve of birth control, but the more likely they were to approve of care centers.

It can also be seen that the higher the percent Black, the less likely officials were to approve of women's rights. This finding is consistent

Table 4.13. Sex-Related Attitudes, by Race, Sex, and Demographic Setting Variables (Percent)[a]

| | Birth Control | | Care Centers | | Women's Rights | | | |
	Black Males	Black Females	Black Males	Black Females	Black Males	Black Females	White Males	White Females
Region								
South	33	56	78	77	48	56	59	*
North	41	42	72	80	64	59	60	72
Population size								
Large	40	52	69	83	66	64	64	*
Small	35	44	79	76	50	49	56	56
Percent Black								
High ·	34	47	80	80	55	52	59	62
Low	41	50	70	75	59	67	62	79

[a]Among Black officials here, the smallest percentage base is 20; the largest is 369. Among White officials, the smallest percentage base is 13; the largest is 248. The first cell indicates that 33 percent of male Black officials in the South favored birth control.

* Base less than 10; too small for percentaging.

Table 4.14. Sex-Related Attitudes, by Race, Sex, and Type of Office (Percent)[a]

| | Birth Control | | Care Centers | | Women's Rights | | | |
Type of office	Black Males	Black Females	Black Males	Black Females	Black Males	Black Females	White Males	White Females
State	33	54	77	100	74	54	65	*
County	32	73	79	83	50	64	50	*
City	41	52	77	70	52	46	55	*
Law	33	*	68	*	65	*	76	*
Education	38	31	72	73	58	66	56	74

[a]Among Black officials here, the smallest percentage base is 11; the largest is 287. Among White officials here, the smallest percentage base is 20; the largest is 164. The first cell indicates that 33 percent of male Black officials who held state office favored birth control.

* Base less than 10, too small for percentaging.

across all categories of respondents shown in Table 4.13, but is especially strong among the females. This suggests that although female Black officials were less likely than male Black officials to experience subjective contradiction between support for racial equality and support for sexual equality, they (and their White counterparts) were less likely to advocate the latter in objective circumstances where the former was more salient. In other words, female officials of both races seem to have suppressed their ordinarily strong interest in women's rights in areas where their electorates were apt to be more insistent on Blacks' rights.

But it should be emphasized that although the inference seems justified from Table 4.13 that heavily Black electorates did not favor (and may have opposed) women's rights, Table 4.2 has clearly shown that Black women (but not White women) were elected to government office more often by such electorates than by less heavily Black electorates, and Table 4.3 has indicated that Black women were not severely confined in the types of office they held. It is as though the more densely Black communities were disposed to support Black women over Black men as protagonists of cross-sexual racial equality, but on the condition that these women did not also become protagonists of cross-racial sexual equality.

With respect to type of office,[3] we found several interesting contrasts and similarities, despite an occasionally trivial case base. For example, although female Black officials at the state level were more favorable toward birth control and care centers as means toward Black progress than were male Black officials at this level, they were less favorable than the men toward women's rights, and female Black city officials were even less favorably inclined. In addition, female Black and White respondents who were law officials agreed in their repudiation of women's rights (relative to the degree of support given by male law officials), while their counterparts among education officials supported these rights more than did the corresponding males. Thus women respondents of both races leaned in opposite directions from their own-race male counterparts in the same type of social control office, thereby producing a two-way division (between male and female officials and between law and education officials) such that male law officials and female education officials were more likely to support women's rights, and female law officials and male education officials were less likely to do so. This contrast persists with respect to the other two attitudes in Table 4.14 (of course, for Black officials only): Female law officials and male education officials gave support to birth control and care centers as means toward Black progress, while male law officials and female education officials withheld it. Indeed, considering our earlier finding regarding the tendencies of law officials to be male and education officials to be female (Table 4.2), it does not seem unreasonable to suggest that our data may reflect some persistent normative tendency in American society to sex-type responsibility for socialization agencies

---

[3] Our case base was too often trivial to justify presenting a table on the role of party affiliation in sex differences on attitude toward birth control as a means toward Black progress. In any case, no consistent party differences were suggested by such data.

as feminine and responsibility for correctional and punitive agencies as masculine.

Moreover, certain attitudes may be normatively designated as differentially appropriate for females and males holding office in masculine-typed and in feminine-typed agencies, and this designation may more unequivocally reflect the overall male domination of American society and culture in the following way: Females in the masculine agency either may be selected (by themselves or by recruiters) for their super-masculinity, or, once in the agency, may become more masculine than the males, as it were. Males in the feminine agency, however, may be protected by the overall sociocultural domination of males from such agency selection or super-conversion and remain more masculine than the surrounding females. Thus, as noted earlier, our data show that females in law enforcement (masculine-typed) agencies were much more likely to oppose women's rights than were males in these agencies. But males in education (feminine-typed) agencies were less likely to support women's rights than were females in these agencies.

CHAPTER 5

Who Helped Elect
Them and Why

Which Constituencies Helped Whom

In our analysis so far, we have examined relationships among characteristics of our respondents and of their environments. Except for the indirect view provided by type of office, however, we have not yet focused on the fact that our respondents were *elected* government officials. So let us now ask: Whom did Black officials (and White officials) think helped them get elected?

To answer this question, we examine officials' perceived election help from four constituencies—the latter term conceived broadly, as groups from which officials receive electoral support (or opposition) of some sort. We consider the Black community and the White community as sources of *votes* for political candidates, and political parties and the mass media as sources of *visibility and certification* for such candidates. We discuss first the sources of visibility and certification.

Among other things, political parties are social institutions through which candidates are selected and publicly certified as "nominees," eligible to receive votes from the electorate at the appointed times and places. Of course, political parties are not the only means of certification. In principle at least, candidates who petition in specified ways may run as "independents" without receiving any party nomination, and candidates may (again, at least in principle) rely solely on the mass media for publicity without utilizing any of the party door-to-door campaign machinery. For their part, the media are sources of visibility both before and after a candidate has received a party nomination or completed his or her petition to run as an independent. The media provide such persons with "exposure" and thereby also with some degree of de facto certification.

But once the procedures of candidate certification and public visibility are underway through party and/or mass media apparatuses, formal decision-making power shifts to the only institution that can legitimately confer elective office—the electorate, the vote-producing constituencies. In the present study, we divide this electorate into two broad communities —Black and White—corresponding to the two racial identification categories into which our respondents are divided.

Thus we conceive a broadly functional (and also structural) relationship between the sources of visibility and of votes such that the former provided means by which our respondents became actually eligible for election, and the latter provided means by which they formally achieved elective office.

Having argued for a functional distinction between sources of visibility and sources of votes, however, it must be added that in the United States of the 1970s, the parties and the media are more closely connected by virtue of their ownership and control to one of the vote sources (namely, the White community) than to the other. In this sense, then, our study may be said to deal with only two electoral constituencies: the Black community, on the one hand, and the White community (including party and media apparatuses that still are under the nearly exclusive control of the latter[1], on the other.

Table 5.1 summarizes the way respondents answered our questions regarding the election help or hindrance they thought they had received from the Black community, the White community, the party to which they were affiliated, and the mass media. Our first Black-White contrast in this respect lies in the finding that when race of official and race of community are taken into account, Black officials consistently thought they received more election help from each sector of each constituency than did White officials. This is easy to see in the party and media data, and it also becomes clear when the Black and White communities are considered as the officials' own-race or other-race communities. Thus, for example, 80 percent of Black officials reported receiving help from their own-race "organizations and leaders not in government," while only 58 percent of White officials did so. Similarly, 58 percent of Black officials said they received help from their other-race "organizations and leaders not in government," while only 32 percent of White comparison officials said this.

---

[1] This is not to deny the existence of Black-owned newspapers, magazines and radio stations that provide access almost exclusively to the Black community.

Table 5.1. Perceived Election Help from Constituencies[a] (Percent)

	Black Officials				White Officials			
	Helped[b]	Neither	Hindered	Total	Helped[b]	Neither	Hindered	Total
Black Community								
Organizations and leaders not in government[c]	80	19	2	100 (678)	32	61	8	100 (378)
Leaders in government[c]	55	42	3	100 (571)	18	76	6	100 (353)
Unorganized population[c]	87	11	2	100 (653)	31	65	4	100 (367)
White Community								
Organizations and leaders not in government[d]	58	35	7	100 (601)	58	40	2	100 (370)
Leaders in government[d]	47	42	10	100 (596)	47	49	4	100 (360)
Unorganized population[d]	56	36	8	100 (623)	69	31	—	100 (372)
Party Apparatus								
Party leaders[e]	66	28	5	100 (640)	56	39	5	100 (384)
Campaign workers[e]	92	8	—	100 (654)	78	22	—	100 (375)
Mass Media[f]	64	32	4	100 (600)	49	47	4	100 (361)

a The ideas for these questions came from Jones (1971).

b Percent "Helped Very Much" plus percent "Helped Somewhat."

c Employed in constructing Index of Black Election Help (BEH).

d Employed in constructing Index of White Election Help (WEH).

e Employed in constructing Index of Party Election Help (PEH).

f The indicator of Media Election Help (MEH).

The race-related discrepancies in these respects may be epitomized by noting that Black officials thought they received as much help from two of the three sectors of the White community as did White officials, but White officials thought they received far less help from all three sectors of the Black community than did Black officials.

Note that Black officials and White officials did not differ radically in their uniformly low perceptions of election hindrance (although Black officials perceived slightly more hindrance from the White community—especially from White leaders in government—than White officials did from the Black community); what seems to have made the difference is the sharply lowered levels of perceived neutrality among all of the Black officials' constituencies. Thus it was not that Black officials perceived their constituencies as harboring less hostility, but rather less neutrality, than did White officials.

Table 5.2 presents the breakdown by region, and we find that Black officials were consistently (though slightly) more likely to believe themselves well-supported by each of their own-race constituency segments inside than outside the South, but were just as consistently more likely to believe themselves well-supported by each of their other-race constitu-

Table 5.2. Perceived Election Help from Constituency Segments Holding
Constant Region (Percent)[a]

	Black Officials		White Officials	
	South	North	South	North
Black Community				
Organizations and leaders				
not in government	85	75	39	24
Leaders in government	59	52	20	16
Unorganized population	91	85	43	21
White Community				
Organizations and leaders				
not in government	51	62	66	50
Leaders in government	43	51	53	43
Party Apparatus				
Party leaders	63	69	53	58
Campaign workers	90	93	74	80
Mass Media	61	65	45	51

[a]Among Black officials here, the smallest percentage base is 219; the largest is 373. Among White officials here, the smallest percentage base is 150; the largest is 220. The first cell indicates that 85 percent of southern Black officials reported a high degree of election help from Black organizations and leaders not in government.

ency segments, as well as by their party and media constituencies, outside than inside the South. White officials agreed with Black officials in thinking they received more election help from their party and media constituencies outside than inside the South. But in contrast to Black officials, they thought more help came from their other-race, as well as their own-race constituency segments, inside than outside the South. The indicated Black-White regional asymmetry seems to mean that Black officials were more supported by the White community where that community had less intensely racist traditions (i.e., outside the South), and by the Black community where that community had had more intense experience with racism (i.e., inside the South). White officials, however, were more acceptable to the Black community, as well as to the White community, where racist traditions and experience were more intense (i.e., inside the South). This appears, indeed, to have been one continuing political mark, in 1971, of White oppression of the Black community: The Black community was still viewed by White officials as more amenable to White leadership where White oppression has been more severe than where it has been less severe. Note that this opinion was strongest with respect to the unorganized, and therefore perhaps the most oppressed, segment of the Black community.

Nevertheless it remains true, in Table 5.2 as in Table 5.1, that Black officials saw themselves as being more secure politically than were White officials, and as facing essentially no tougher political resistance in any constituency sector than they did. The picture is sanguine indeed for a racial group so long effectively barred from holding government office.

How is this finding to be explained? There seem to be only two possibilities: Either Black officials' constituencies actually *were* more supportive of them and the finding merely reflects that objective fact, or these constituencies were *not* more supportive of them and the finding reflects some other, subjective fact. Unfortunately, our data provide no direct way of choosing between these alternatives. But one item of indirect evidence is worth pursuing: 51 percent of Black respondents had won only one election in their careers; only 30 percent of White respondents fell into that category, and 45 percent of them had won three or more elections, as compared with 25 percent of Black officials. In short, when compared with the White officials in our sample, the Black officials were political novices. Under these circumstances, it would hardly be surprising if Black officials' initial successes in an arena to which even entrance had so long been denied them were to produce sanguine evaluations of the entire environment there—a psychologically buoyant effect of what might be called initial relative equalization. To the extent that this hypothesis is true, we would expect Black officials' buoyancy to decrease as their political experience increased.[2] But to the extent that constituencies actually gave greater election help to Black than to White officials, we would expect no such decreases—indeed, perhaps an increase—in Black officials' perceptions of constituency helpfulness.

But the measure at our disposal—number of elections won—undoubtedly reflects political *exposure to* the electorate as well as political *experience with* the electorate. Consequently, our general expectation is that perceived election help from every constituency segment will correlate positively with this measure. In other words, we expect that all officials, regardless of their race, who were objectively better known to their constituencies from victorious campaigns in the past had a better chance of getting election help from those constituencies than did officials with less auspicious election records. But if the hypothesis of a subjective difference between the races with respect to equalization buoyancy is true, then Black officials should show less of an increase in perceived election help with the same increase in number of elections won than White officials (i.e., the associations between these two variables should be less positive among Black officials than among their White counterparts).

Table 5.3 presents the data, and we find that with three exceptions

Table 5.3. Associations Between Perceived Election Help from Constituency Segments and Numbers of Elections Won (Yule's Q)

	South		North	
	Black	White	Black	White
Black Community				
Organizations and leaders				
not in government	.14	.32	−.42	−.03
Leaders in government	.22	.41	−.12	−.15
Unorganized population	.41	.57	.10	.09
White Community				
Organizations and leaders				
not in government	.10	.20	−.02	.22
Leaders in government	.18	.31	.14	.32
Unorganized population	.26	.21	.08	.24
Party Apparatus				
Party leaders	.21	.22	−.44	.36
Campaign workers	.40	−.08	.35	.19
Mass Media	−.02	−.12	−.06	.20

[2] Indeed, one may imagine a damped oscillation from optimistic to pessimistic evaluations as experience increases. Thus, culture shock may induce an alternating, and fading, current among those who are being acculturated.

in the South, and two exceptions outside the South, the hypothesis is confirmed; there is good reason to think that at least some of the Black-White difference in perceived election help shown in Table 5.1 was subjectively inflationary on the part of Black officials, and attributable to their inexperience with political constituencies. Even the only major departure from this pattern (i.e., the finding that Black officials in both regions reported substantially greater increases in election help from campaign workers than did White officials with the same increase in electoral successes) seems consistent with Black officials' newness to politics. That is, it is conceivable that potential campaign workers (especially young ones) could more enthusiastically give their loyalty to a new, and successful, brand of candidate than to an old, even though more successful, brand of candidate. But as (and if) the presence of Black officials in government becomes more common and more taken for granted over the years to come, we would expect this novelty to wear off, and the initial bandwagon inflation of campaign worker support will then decline toward the levels observed among White officials.

It is interesting to note, however, as an aside, that the more elections Black (and to some extent, White) officials outside the South had won, the more support they perceived from the unorganized segments of the Black community there. In fact, these Black officials seem to have thought that electoral success brought relative isolation from most of their constituency segments—with certain interesting exceptions. The exceptions were, first of all, their campaign workers; second, White leaders in government; and finally the unorganized populations of the Black and White communities. It is as though electorally successful northern Black officials thought they built up (1) personal followings that bypassed party leaders in reaching the unorganized populations of the White as well as the Black communities and (2) alliances with White government leaders that tended to exclude other Black leaders—especially nongovernment ones.

Returning to Table 5.2, note that Black and White officials seem generally to have agreed on the first few ranks in evaluating their sources of election help. Ranking from the most powerful to the least powerful sources, these were (with some small variation between regions) campaign workers, own-race unorganized populations, own-race organization and leaders not in government, party leaders, and mass media. Both Black and White officials also agreed in assigning the bottom, least helpful rank to other-race leaders in government. This seems likely to have been a sign of intense pre-election competition between such leaders and themselves (a competition, however, that Table 5.9 will show probably gave way to a growing political cooperation after elections).

Further, higher proportions of both groups of officials (especially the

White) said they were helped more by the "unorganized" populations in their own-race communities than by either "organizations or leaders not in government" or "leaders in government." This was not the case with respect to perceived help from the other-race communities; there, as much or slightly more support was thought to have come from "organizations and leaders not in government." This seems to suggest that officials of both races thought of themselves as more successfully appealing primarily to the "grass roots" in their own-race communities, but to the "leadership" in their other-race communities. It is as though they had to go more "through channels" abroad, but could go more "directly to the people" at home.

   Table 5.2 is still relatively close to the raw data, and the variables shown are much too detailed for easy management in the analysis to follow. We therefore combined respondents' estimates of the help or hindrance they received from each sector shown in Table 5.1 into simple indexes of perceived election help or hindrance from each of the four constituencies discussed earlier—namely, the party and mass media appara-

Table 5.4. Percent High on Indexes of Perceived Election Help[a]

| | Black Officials | | White Officials | |
	South	North	South	North
BEH[b]	47	37	47	29
WEH[c]	41	59	66	52
PEH[d]	40	50	54	65
MEH[e]	46 (317)	54 (416)	36 (188)	44 (239)

   [a]All indexes were constructed by scoring "Helped Very Much" = 4; "Helped Somewhat" = 3; "Neither Helped nor Hindered" = 2; "Mainly Hindered" = 1. The simple sum of these scores across the appropriate questions, as indicated in Table 5.1, constituted the indexes. Missing values were provided individual items in the BEH, WEH, and PEH sets of questions by assigning the neutral response ("Neither Helped nor Hindered"), provided that the respondent had answered at least one question in the set.

   [b] Scores on this index dichotomized at > 9 for Black officials (range 3–12), at > 6 for White officials (range 3–12).

   [c] Scores on this index dichotomized at > 8 for all respondents (range 3–12).

   [d] Scores on this index dichotomized at > 7 for all respondents (range 2–8).

   [e] Responses on this indicator dichotomized at "Helped Very Much" plus "Helped Somewhat" versus "Neither Helped nor Hindered" plus "Mainly Hindered."

tuses and the Black and White communities. We termed these summary measures BEH (Black Election Help), WEH (White Election Help), PEH (Party Election Help), and MEH (Media Election Help). These indexes constitute the focus of analysis for the rest of this chapter.

Because the Black-White differences with respect to perceived help from segments of the Black community constituency (shown in Table 5.1) were so great, we dichotomized the Black election help index at its race-specific medians, but the White election help index and the party election help index were dichotomized at their overall medians; and the media indicator was dichotomized for all respondents by grouping "Helped Very Much" plus "Helped Somewhat" together versus "Neither Helped nor Hindered" and "Mainly Hindered." This means that the percentages referring to BEH are not comparable across race of official; percentages referring to all other election help indexes are comparable. Our measure of association (Yule's Q), of course, continues to be comparable across race of official as well as otherwise, and we will employ such figures in much of our analysis.

Table 5.4 presents some information concerning the dichotomous distributions of these indexes, holding constant region. The regional and racial differences shown here may be typified by imagining an average Black official and an average White official moving their permanent residences from the northern to the southern region. The White official's total perceived political gains would be relatively greater than those of the Black official, insofar as the former would experience a proportionately larger gain in help from the other-race community and he or she would also gain help from the own-race community, whereas the Black official would lose help from the other-race community. Both Black and White officials, of course, would perceive a loss of help from their political parties and from the mass media.

Election Help Relationships among Constituencies

Now let us turn to more complex substantive questions. From our conceptualization of the party and media apparatuses and the Black and White communities as sources of visibility and of votes, respectively, a series of questions arise on which our data can cast some light: To what extent was election help (presumably including votes) in the Black and White communities perceived, by Black and by White officials, as influenced by the party and media apparatuses? To put this question crudely one might ask which apparatus (if either) was believed to "deliver" which vote. To what extent were the Black and White communities perceived as mutually complementary help-producing entities? Similarly, to what extent were the party and media apparatuses perceived as mutually complementary in producing electoral visibility? These questions are special forms of the more general one: How were perceptions about help and hindrance from the four constituencies related to each other?

An approach to this question is presented in Table 5.5. One striking finding here is that the associations are generally lower in the North than in the South. This is more true among Black officials than among White, and there is one clear exception among the latter (PEH), but in general it appears that elected government officials of both races were likely to perceive their four constituencies as more independent of each other outside the South. The data in this case reflect a commonplace observation, that the South is politically more "solid" or "bloc-like" than the North.

Table 5.5. Interrelationships of Election Help Indexes (Yule's Q)

| | South | | | North | | |
	WEH	PEH	MEH	WEH	PEH	MEH
			Black Officials			
BEH	.28	.50	.35	.18	.24	.08
WEH		.53	.64		.35	.49
PEH			.60			.37
			White Officials			
BEH	.45	.18	.36	.46	.53	.24
WEH		.72	.61		.39	.47
PEH			.68			.54

Beyond this general regional difference in relationships between constituencies, however, note the suggestion of these data that Black election help was more independent of the party and media apparatuses (with one exception among northern White officials) than White election help. This appears to have been the opinion of White as well as Black respondents, and in the South as well as in the North. Before continuing with Table 5.5, let us pause to explore this finding further, because it promises to answer our question concerning the "deliverability" of the Black and White vote by party and/or media apparatuses.

In Table 5.6 it can be seen, with both party and media sources held constant, that southern Black officials seem to have believed (1) that election support from the Black community was notably more closely related to party than to media support; and (2) that the reverse was true of election support from the White community. Southern White officials seem to have held just the opposite of these views. Outside the South, Black officials agreed with their southern Black counterparts, though the relation-

Table 5.6. Perceived Black Election Help (BEH), and White Election Help (WEH), Holding Constant Party Election Help (PEH), and Media Election Help (MEH) (Percent)[a]

| | South PEH | | | | North PEH | | | |
| | Low MEH | | High MEH | | Low MEH | | High MEH | |
	Low	High	Low	High	Low	High	Low	High
				Black Officials				
BEH	33	42	55	68	26	34	43	45
WEH	19	50	39	67	44	59	48	79
				White Officials				
BEH	39	53	41	60	10	32	38	35
WEH	41	67	78	89	32	50	52	67

[a]Among Black officials here, the smallest percentage base is 44; the largest is 130. Among White officials, the smallest percentage base is 15; the largest is 85. The first cell indicates that 33 percent of southern Black officials who reported low PEH and low MEH reported high BEH.

ships are not as strong, while White officials gave roughly equal weight to party and media apparatuses in relation to support from the Black and the White communities. Our data suggest, then, that in the South Black officials and White officials thought their own-race community electorates were more party-delivered and their other-race community electorates were more media-delivered. But outside the South, the two sources of visibility were judged more nearly equal (especially by White officials) in their influence on the two sources of votes. This regional difference could have resulted from southern officials' more racially segregated familiarity with their party's activities in their own-race communities than in their other-race communities, plus a tendency to attribute any residual effect on their other-race communities to the mass media to which Black and White alike were known to be exposed. This finding provides an interesting supplement to the suggestion made earlier (based on Table 5.2) that our respondents may have thought themselves more successful in eliciting support from the unorganized than from the organized segments of their own-race communities, but the reverse in their other-race communities. The finding just noted suggests the additional possibility that southern officials may have thought of the party apparatus as the chief means for eliciting help directly from the unorganized segments of their own-race communities and considered the media as the chief means for doing so from the organized segments of their other-race communities.

From our evidence, it seems fair to conclude that the northern officials in our sample thought that their constituencies were more loosely bound together and that the vote was much less influenced by party or media apparatuses, than did southern officials. (As we have indicated, this was especially the case for Black officials' perceptions of the Black vote.) To the extent to which northern officials did perceive the vote as influenced by either apparatus, however, it appears that they generally thought of the Black vote as more closely tied to the party apparatus and the White vote as more closely tied to the media apparatus.

Now returning to Table 5.5, it should be pointed out that the association between perceived election help from the Black community and perceived election help from the White community was much less close, in the North as well as the South, among Black than among White officials. In other words, Black officials were more likely than White officials to think the Black community and the White community constituted independent, rather than connected, sources of help. Black officials also perceived weaker associations between party and media election support than did White officials. Again, this suggests that Black officials were less likely to think of these apparatuses as connected. In general, then, the independence of constituencies seems to have been more characteristic of Black officials' than of White officials' perceptions. Black officials may have felt themselves engaged in more of a structurally segmented fight, where they had won (or lost) each constituency separately; White officials may have felt greater structural interdependence among their constituencies—winning (or losing) them all more or less as a bloc. That Black officials also saw less temporal continuity in the help their constituencies gave them will be discussed next.

Election Help and Incumbency Help

One way of characterizing a community said to be behaving politically as a "bloc" is structural, and another way is temporal. In the first case, all sectors of the community vote for the same candidate, whereas in the second case, once they have elected such a candidate, they then give him or her their continuous and exclusive support. Our data do not provide any means for examining actual or perceived voting unanimity in either the Black or the White community. But we do have a means of casting some light on the extent to which support was perceived to have been continuous over time, and Table 5.7 presents some of the relevant data. In this table only, we introduce a new variable: the index of perceived incumbency help (IH), which was constructed in the same way as the election help index but from questions that asked respondents to evaluate

Table 5.7. Interrelationships Between Black and White Community Election
Help (EH) and Incumbency Help (IH) (Yule's Q)

| | South | | North | |
	BEH	WEH	BEH	WEH
		Black Officials		
BIH	.55	.04	.34	.07
WIH	.21	.61	—.06	.57
		White Officials		
BIH	.71	.39	.68	.38
WIH	.50	.53	.40	.44

the helpfulness of constituencies and their segments with respect to the officials' "performance of duties in their present office."

Table 5.7 indicates that all officials believed that receiving substantial election help from either the Black or the White community constituted a strong promise of incumbency help from that community, but much less so from the other community. For example, among Black officials in the South the associations between election help and incumbency help within the Black community and the White community, respectively, are shown to be .55 and .61. The associations of election help and incumbency help between the two communities, however, were only .21 and .04. Although this is clearly the pattern throughout the four parts of the table, the within-community versus between-community differences are considerably greater among Black officials than among White. This seems to confirm the suggestion of Table 5.5 that Black officials were inclined to perceive the Black and White communities as independent, perhaps mutually exclusive or antagonistic, sources of support, while White officials tended to perceive these constituencies as more interconnected, perhaps mutually cooperating, sources of support.

Another way of putting this conclusion, of course, is to say that Black officials were more likely to believe that their constituencies, Black and White, defined them as specialized representatives of Black people, rather than as generalized representatives of the people at large. This belief has already been documented by interview comments presented earlier. Thus, when Black officials believed strong support came from the White community, they were likely to believe, in addition, that they were denied the incumbency support from the Black community that comparable White officials were much more likely to receive. The reverse situation was also present: When Black officials thought they received strong election support from the Black community, they were also likely to think that the White community shunned them, denying them incumbency support.

Thus it seems that having Black support led Black officials to believe the White community thought them "not to be trusted" as representatives of White people and that having White support led them to believe the Black community thought them "traitors to the race." The White counterparts of these Black officials apparently did not labor under either of these constraining political consequences of racial identity and could think of themselves as more race-free in the eyes of their Black, as well as of their White, constituencies.

It is also noteworthy, and somewhat surprising, that both racial groups of officials thought support from their other-race community was more continuous than support from their own-race community (i.e., the magnitudes of other-race EH:IH associations were greater than those of own-race associations). But our data also show, more expectedly, that own-race communities were thought to offer more continuity inside than outside the South, with the result that the difference between the perceived continuity of the two communities was less inside than outside the South. In other words, the two racial electorates were thought to have been more or less evenly matched with respect to race-related continuity of support inside the South; outside the South, the other-race electorate was thought to offer even more continuity than the own-race electorate. And it is important to add that this last point was true not because of any difference in other-race continuity between the regions, but because of a lowered own-race continuity outside the South.

We can see in Table 5.7 that, with one exception, every association among White officials was stronger than the corresponding one among Black officials. This suggests that White officials saw more continuity over time (as well as unity at a given point in time, as Table 5.5 indicated) in perceived support from their electorates than did Black officials. The latter seem to have thought themselves engaged not only in a structurally segmented trial but in a temporally discontinuous, round-by-round one as well. The exception to this generalization lies in the associations between election help and incumbency help from the White constituency; these are somewhat stronger in both regions, but especially outside the South, among Black officials than among White officials. Perhaps this is a statistical reflection of the development by Black officials of White "followings" —as expressed by one northern Black interviewee.

> The notion that Black leaders can lead White people was new to me and one that I had not agreed with when I first took office. I thought that we could move White leaders to lead White people, but it is now becoming clear that the position in which Black leadership finds itself—that it's now developing White followers.

Table 5.8. Interrelationships Between Party and Media Election Help and
Incumbency Help (Yule's Q)

	South		North	
	PEH	MEH	PEH	MEH
		Black Officials		
PIH	.57	.45	.59	.08
MIH	.32	.70	.29	.57
		White Officials		
PIH	.61	.65	.86	.41
MIH	.55	.74	.41	.75

In general, however, Black officials seem to have viewed their constituencies as attitudinally less indifferent to them (see Table 5.1), structurally more segmented, and temporally less continuous than did White
officials—all of which perceptions may be typical of controversial newcomers to the political scene.

Now let us deal with the exchange between official and constituency: To what extent did officials return something to their constituencies for the election help they reported receiving from them?

While we have no direct evidence on this question, we do have some
indirect evidence, since we asked each respondent to estimate the extent
to which he or she had made friends or enemies among the various constituencies after having been elected. If we assume that in order to make
friends in a certain constituency an official generally had to do something
(whether in word or deed, or both) for that constituency, our respondents'
answers to this question may be combined with their estimates of help in
getting elected to give us a measure of political *quid pro quo*—i.e., a measure of the extent to which perceived election help *from* a given constituency was viewed as successfully reciprocated by officials' help *to* that
constituency ("successfully" by virtue of the official having then received
friendship in return for his or her help).

Of course, the qualifier "whether in word or deed, or both" is important because persons have been known to win friends solely on the basis
of their words—their verbal pledges, denunciations, "raps," and innuen-
does. So we cannot be sure that some of our officials did not craftily
"sweet-talk" their constituencies into friendliness—or clumsily "mis-
speak" them into hostility. Still, words are deeds, and "telling them what
they want to hear" can repay a constituency for more tangible help in getting an official elected—at least temporarily.[3] In any case, the extent to
which an official thought he had made friends rather than enemies in a

---

[3] Walton (1972:207) refers to "rhetoric politicians."

Table 5.9. Election Help Received from,[a] and Political Help Given to,[b]
Constituency Sectors

	Black Officials			White Officials		
	Help Received	Help Given	Difference[c]	Help Received	Help Given	Difference
Black Community						
Organized leaders						
not in government	80 (678)	62 (719)	−23	32 (378)	42 (405)	+15
Leaders in government	55 (571)	69 (671)	+31	18 (353)	39 (383)	+26
Unorganized population	87 (653)	69 (695)	−21	31 (367)	38 (403)	+10
White Community						
Organized leaders						
not in government	58 (601)	38 (668)	−35	58 (370)	46 (403)	−21
Leaders in government	47 (596)	44 (691)	− 6	47 (360)	53 (409)	+11
Unorganized population	56 (623)	34 (670)	−39	69 (372)	50 (416)	−28
Party Apparatus						
Party leaders	66 (640)	60 (702)	− 9	56 (384)	51 (407)	− 9
Campaign workers	92 (654)	78 (627)	−15	78 (375)	60 (386)	−23
Mass Media	64 (600)	51 (633)	−20	49 (361)	45 (394)	− 8

[a] Percent "Helped," from Table 5.1.

[b] Percent "Made Mostly Friends" responses to following question: "On the whole, do you think you have made mostly friends or mostly enemies among the following individuals and groups as a result of being an elected official—Made Mostly Friends; Made Mostly Enemies; Made Both Friends and Enemies; Made neither Friends nor Enemies?" See text for interpretation as "Help Given."

[c] The "Effectiveness Index" of Hovland et al. (1949:284–292). This measure is the increase or decrease in percent taken as a percent of the total possible increase or decrease. Thus for the first figure in the "Black Officials" column, we have (80−62)/ 80=−23. The standardization controls for differences among the initial percentages.

given constituency seems likely to reflect the net balance of things he or she had done and said for and against that constituency.

Consider, therefore, Table 5.9 where we show the percent saying they had "made mostly friends" in a given constituency sector and the standardized percent difference between that figure and the percent saying they had received help in getting elected from the same sector (taken from Table 5.1.). Note first that although Black leaders in government ranked very low (eighth) in election help given to Black officials, they ranked very high (second or third) in political help received by them from Black officials. Similarly, White leaders in government were ranked sixth in election help given to White officials, but second in political help received from White officials. These major shifts in rank help to account for the important finding that the percent difference between election help received and political help given was larger for leaders in the government sector than for any other sector of officials' own-race constituencies; indeed, it was the only positive difference in all the constituencies of Black officials. Still more generally, leaders in the government sector show the most positive (or least negative, in one case) percent difference of all sectors in the other-race, as well as the own-race, constituencies.

These findings may well reflect the process of collegial group-formation among elected government officials—primarily within-race, but between-races as well—since our data show that both Black and White officials saw themselves as being drawn more rapidly toward their governmental colleagues than to other parts of their political environments. Such collegial solidarity is attributable to at least two different (but not exclusive) initiatives, even though we have no way, in this study, of estimating their separate effects. Thus oldtimers may have exercised the initiative called "recruitment," while newcomers may have exercised the initiative called "invasion." In the first case, although leaders who were already in government may not have enthusiastically supported the many untried candidates wishing to enter government, they may have voluntarily sought out the election winners as they took office and welcomed them into colleagueship. In the second case, candidates for government office, sensitive to election help or lack of it from their seniors already in government, may have set out after their elections to repay that help or assuage that hostility and thereby win their way into the oldtimers' colleagueship.

But there is at least one other, equally important, finding in Table 5.9: The percent differences of White officials toward the Black community are uniformly positive—and, with one minor exception, more so than those of Black officials—while the percent differences of Black officials toward the White community are uniformly negative and more so than those of White officials. This suggests that Black officials did not think they repaid help received with help given to the same extent as did White officials—and this may again reflect the newness of Black officials and their relative lack of control over patronage and other prerequisites of long incumbency.

However, despite these processes, it remains true that Black officials registered higher levels of political help given to all three sectors of the Black community than did White officials in the White community. Together, these findings suggest that Black officials saw themselves as much closer (insofar as "closeness" is measured in Table 5.9) to the Black community—including its nongovernmental sectors—than did White officials.

Why Constituencies Helped

We come now to the last major question to which our survey data are applied here, namely, What were some of the personal background, social setting, and attitudinal correlates of perceived election help? In other words, What kinds of Black elected officials, in what settings, holding what ideologies, etc., were helped (or hindered) most by which constituencies?

Personal Background

As one might well expect, the more memberships an official held in voluntary associations, the more election help he or she received from every constituency (Table 5.10). But it is interesting to note that in the South, such membership correlated more strongly with election help from own-race communities than with election help from other-race communities. Outside the South this was clearly less true—especially for White officials. The findings on age, on the other hand, are generally the reverse of these: The associations of age with election help from own-race communities were uniformly weaker than those with help from other-race communities. Together, these findings seem best interpreted as reflections of the separation of Black and White communities in both regions. Given this condition it seems understandable that officials should have participated in voluntary organizations within their own-race community, and have, on this basis, elicited election support there. In the other-race community, however, age—simple duration of experience—may have carried as much or more weight. At the same time, it should be noted that the age associations (with two minor exceptions) are weaker than the corresponding membership associations—suggesting that range of experience generally carried more weight with these officials' several constituencies than duration of experience.

It is also interesting that the only constituencies that tended to favor youth over age were the party and mass media apparatuses, where such characteristics as "glamor" and "audacity" may count more than "experience" and "maturity."

With respect to the bearings of officials' residence and education on perceived election help, we find that education was positively associated with election help from the Black community and from the mass media throughout all categories of respondents, and it was also positively associated with election help from the White community among Black officials (although it was negatively associated among northern White officials). Residence, however, seems to have had the same kind of relationship to

Table 5.10. Associations Between Perceived Election Help and Residence, Education, Age, and Membership (Yule's Q)

	South				North			
	Residence	Education	Age	Memberships	Residence	Education	Age	Memberships
				Black Officials				
BEH	-.13	.24	.07	.39	.07	.25	.09	.27
WEH	.15	.34	.16	.20	.20	.20	.19	.23
PEH	.13	-.01	-.06	.24	.20	.11	.20	.27
MEH	-.21	.28	-.30	.42	.04	.06	-.06	.31
				White Officials				
BEH	.23	.07	.29	.06	.32	.32	.36	.32
WEH	-.01	.09	.11	.40	-.06	-.18	.17	.18
PEH	-.32	.25	-.16	.30	.37	-.14	-.08	.52
MEH	.08	.22	-.02	.47	-.06	.26	.08	.31

perceived election help as did age: It mattered more to election help from the other-race community than from one's own-race community. Both age and residence, then, seem to have been employed as electoral criteria by the community that was less directly familiar with the official.

Now, let us take up a discussion that we began in connection with Table 3.6 regarding the possibility that different implications of memberships were favored in different electoral contexts. Consider Table 5.11: Memberships tended consistently to weigh heavily in determining perceived election help from an official's *own*-race community when that official had relatively low educational attainment or relatively long-time residence. On the other hand, memberships tended (somewhat less consistently) to weigh heavily in determining help from an official's *other*-race community when the official had relatively high educational attainment, or relatively short-time residence. In other words, an official (Black or White) seems to have made better use of memberships in eliciting strong election help from his own-race community if he already had a strong localism identification (i.e., low education or high residence). It seems likely then that in the eyes of an official's own-race community, memberships served not as a complement but as a counterbalance to strong localism. The reverse seems to have been the case for the other-race community: Here memberships served to counterbalance strong cosmopolitanism (i.e., high education or low residence).

Since from the point of view of the Black and the White communities an official is either a racial insider or outsider, these observations may be generalized one step further: It is as though each community, desiring elements of both localism and cosmopolitanism in officials, took for granted the localism of racial insiders and the cosmopolitanism of racial outsiders, and each community rewarded officials for showing positive evidence of whichever characteristic it could not take for granted.

Table 5.11. Associations Between Memberships and Perceived Election Help from the Black and from the White Communities, by Education and Residence (Yule's Q)

| | South | | | | North | | | |
| | Education | | Residence | | Education | | Residence | |
	Low	High	Low	High	Low	High	Low	High
				Black Officials				
BEH	.35	.18	.12	.52	.31	.04	.19	.36
WEH	.16	.41	.26	.28	.10	.31	.16	.28
				White Officials				
BEH	.10	.31	.27	−.12	.29	.17	.28	.33
WEH	.54	.34	.26	.56	.14	.14	.16	.54

That those quite different evidences could have been indicated by the same variable, namely, number of memberships in voluntary associations, seems due to the wide variety of such associations that are available in American life. This makes it possible, to cite the extreme case, for one citizen to belong to a large number of organizations having local interests and another, living in the same community, to belong to an equally large number of organizations having cosmopolitan interests.

But granting that memberships *could* have a variable local or cosmopolitan significance, there seem to be at least two ways that that possibility could become actual (unfortunately, we have no way in this research of assessing them). In one of these, the local and the cosmopolitan implications of memberships may be differentially attributed to officials by their own-race and other-race communities as those communities perceive the officials. In the other, the differential emphasis may be more actively "projected" by the officials themselves than attributed by the communities. That is, candidates and officials might join organizations and select the local or cosmopolitan focus of their activity on the basis of what they need to "round-out" their public images.

Regarding the impact of sex identification on election help, Table 5.12 indicates that although differences were not great among officials of either race, White male officials consistently thought they received more election help from their constituencies than did White female officials. Such sex differences among Black officials, however, appear to have been smaller (with one exception) and, indeed, effectively zero. Thus it seems that one's sex mattered more, with respect to perceived election help, if one were White than if one were Black. In line with these race-related differences, note also that the only constituency whose election help was perceived by Black officials as contingent upon sex was the White community.

Party Affiliation

Our next inquiry pertains to the relationship between party affiliation and perceived election help. Table 5.13 shows (not unexpectedly) that in

Table 5.12. Percent High Perceived Election Help, by Sex

| | Black Officials | | White Officials | |
	Males	Females	Males	Females
BEH	42	40	38	27
WEH	51	42	58	50
PEH	45	44	61	46
MEH	50 (654)	52 (80)	41 (401)	31 (26)

both regions Democratic officials of both races were more likely to be supported by the Black community than were Republican officials, while Republican officials of both races were more likely to be supported by the White community than were Democratic officials—with the exception of northern White officials among whom support from the White community slightly favored Democrats. The moral of this table might be: If you are a Black official and you want maximum support from the Black community, be a southern Democrat; but if you want maximum support from the White community, be a northern Republican.

Table 5.13. Percent High Perceived Election Help, by Party Affiliation

	South			North		
	Democrat	Republican	Other	Democrat	Republican	Other
	Black Officials					
BEH	50	44	33	40	23	43
WEH	41	62	30	53	79	68
PEH	40	44	39	51	52	29
MEH	47 (225)	50 (16)	44 (46)	52 (306)	61 (82)	54 (28)
	White Officials					
BEH	54	35	21	43	17	15
WEH	63	72	71	54	49	50
PEH	48	76	36	75	57	45
MEH	34 (128)	46 (46)	21 (14)	48 (112)	43 (107)	35 (20)

Note also that Black officials of "Other" affiliation reported more help from the Black and the White communities in northern than southern election districts. The finding that southern White officials of "Other" affiliation were much more likely to report help from the White community than from the Black community may be at least partly accounted for by the finding of Table 3.20 that these officials were decidedly hereditarian and therefore, considering that they were White, probably racist and overtly so. On the other hand, the finding that northern White officials of "Other" affiliation were also much more likely to report help from the White community than from the Black community may be partly explained by the finding of Table 3.20 that these officials were even more rightist than other White officials and therefore far to the right of Black officials.

Type of Office

As shown in Table 5.14, we find that among southern Black officials county level office may have been a kind of "hot seat," because if such officials received election help from the Black community, their chances of

Table 5.14. Percent High Perceived Election Help, by Type of Office

	South					North				
	State	County	City	Education	Law	State	County	City	Education	Law
Black Officials										
BEH	58	61	44	30	48	42	29	38	44	34
WEH	55	29	45	29	37	60	54	52	73	63
PEH	48	61	37	39	37	65	46	48	69	36
MEH	77 (31)	36 (31)	47 (161)	27 (33)	48 (60)	62 (52)	44 (41)	52 (149)	56 (52)	53 (122)
White Officials										
BEH	35	80	52	47	33	30	*	37	68	13
WEH	76	70	70	65	42	59	*	63	64	34
PEH	85	50	46	71	39	94	*	78	86	32
MEH	50 (34)	30 (10)	34 (94)	41 (17)	27 (33)	46 (46)	* (6)	59 (73)	64 (22)	26 (93)

* Base less than 10, too small for percentaging.

receiving help from the White community were seriously diminished, and vice versa. Officials at the state and city levels of legislative-executive office do not seem to have experienced these conflicts of support quite as sharply. In the North, we find no strong or systematic relationships between the legislative-executive types of office and perceived election help from any constituency, except that both the parties and the media gave somewhat more election help to Black officials at the state level than at any other level. Among northern White respondents we find that although officials at the city level received somewhat more Black election help than did officials at other levels, county level officials received more help from the White community, the parties, and the media.

Turning now to the social control officials, we find a strikingly consistent relationship: Southern Black law officials were less likely to report election help from three of their constituencies than were education officials. In contrast with this, however, we find that northern Black law officials were more likely to receive election help from their constituencies than were Black education officials. Nevertheless, with a single exception, Black law officials were less likely to say they were supported by any given constituency (including the Black community itself) than were White officials in the same region and same type of office. The contrast in this respect is particularly striking in the South.

Education officials reveal exactly the opposite relationships: Black education officials, in both regions, were more likely to say they received election help from each constituency than were their White counterparts. In fact, White education officials showed the same uniformly negative associations with perceived election help from each constituency that southern Black law officials revealed. The lack of support that White education officials reported is especially great in the North.

Thus Black law enforcement officials considered themselves less well-supported by their constituencies than did their White counterparts; but (also relative to their White counterparts), Black education officials considered themselves better supported by their constituencies. In Chapter 4, we suggested that education and law offices may have been *sex*-typed by the several constituencies such that the former were identified as more appropriate for women and the latter as more appropriate for men. The data in Table 5.14 suggest a complement to this speculation: Education and law types of office may also have been *race*-typed, in the sense that education and law offices may have been held differentially appropriate for Blacks and Whites. One gets the impression that officials of both races thought their electorates held two unreconstructed stereotypic images: the nurturant (educating) Black female and the disciplinarian (judging and law-enforcing) White male.

Ideologies

In looking into the impact of ideologies on perceived election help, consider Table 5.15, where reading across the rows will indicate the ideological correlates of perceived election help from each constituency, and reading down the columns will give the election help correlates of each ideology.

Perhaps the first thing to note here is the generally low level of association between ideologies and perceived election help. In the data on Black officials, 16 of the 32 associations are .10 or less, whereas only 7 out of 32 associations between personal background characteristics and perceived election help (Table 5.10) were that weak. It may be that although, as we noted in Chapter 2, what is inside an official's head probably does more than his or her outside appearance to determine how the duties and rights of office are actually carried out, the reverse may be the case in determining whether he or she gets elected.

As a result, there are only a few associations in Table 5.15 that are strong enough to be noteworthy. Thus we find that Black officials in both regions reported more election help from the White community if they were integrationist or preferred conventional-action than if they advocated Black independence or direct-action. Their hereditarianism or liberalism seems to have mattered little to the White community. On the other hand, liberalism was an asset in eliciting help from the Black community in the North, where preferences for direct-action and Black independence were also assets—though not powerful ones. In the context of contrasts drawn earlier between party and media apparatuses, it is also interesting to see that among Black officials in both regions tendencies toward hereditarianism, conservatism, and preference for conventional-action were assets in eliciting help from the party apparatus, but (relatively speaking) they were liabilities in eliciting help from the media apparatus. Note also that Black officials who advocated Black independence received slightly more support than did integrationist officials only in the North, and only from the Black community there, and that hereditarian White officials were more successful in the White communities of both regions than were non-hereditarians (but less successful in the Black communities there).

Sex-Related Attitudes

Regarding the bearing of the three sex-related issues discussed in Chapter 4 on perceived election help, Table 5.16 reveals a striking general pattern: Female officials believed they lost election support, if they held

Table 5.15. Associations Between Ideologies and Perceived Election Help (Yule's Q)

	South				North			
	Hereditarianism	Direct-Action	Independence	Liberalism	Hereditarianism	Direct-Action	Independence	Liberalism
Black Officials								
BEH	−.07	−.03	−.10	.01	.00	.18	.11	.43
WEH	−.08	−.19	−.32	−.09	−.05	−.17	−.32	−.05
PEH	.03	−.07	.00	−.18	.11	−.23	−.37	−.04
MEH	−.22	−.02	−.05	.21	−.03	.10	−.12	.13
White Officials								
BEH	−.06			−.16	.05			.36
WEH	.27			−.19	.21			−.07
PEH	−.09			.00	.05			.20
MEH	−.02			.13	−.05			.23

favorable attitudes toward these issues far more often than did male officials. Of the twelve coefficients shown in this table, only two of those computed for male Black officials are negative; nine of those computed for female Black officials are negative. Moreover, in eight out of twelve cross-sex comparisons among Black officials the absolute magnitude of coefficients computed for females is larger than that of coefficients computed for males—suggesting that attitudes toward the sex-related issues generally had a greater impact, whether for reward or punishment (though mostly the latter), on the electoral fortunes of women. Apparently, it was not generally part of woman's place to defend herself.

Table 5.16. Associations Between Attitudes Toward Sex-Related Issues and Perceived Election Help, by Sex (Yule's Q)

| | Attitudes | | | | | | | |
| | Birth Control | | Care Centers | | Women's Rights | | | |
	Black Males	Black Females	Black Males	Black Females	Black Males	Black Females	White Males	White Females
BEH	.04	—.26	.05	.25	.08	—.59	.02	.63
WEH	.27	—.20	—.14	—.42	.10	.08	.04	.18
PEH	.05	.02	.00	—.01	.10	—.28	.06	—.29
MEH	.06	—.31	—.11	—.09	.16	—.31	.04	.70

On examining the findings of Table 5.16 on each attitude separately, we find that although support for women's rights had little bearing on the election help that male Black or White officials perceived from any constituency, such support sometimes bore quite heavily on the election help that female Black, and White, officials perceived. The direction of that effect, however, differed between Black and White female officials, such that, although the former perceived a decided loss of support from the Black community and from the mass media if they believed in women's rights, the latter seem to have gained considerable support from both of these constituencies for that belief. On the other hand, both female Black officials and their White counterparts thought they lost support from their parties and gained support, slightly, from the White community, if they believed in women's rights.

In general then, Table 5.16 seems to suggest that elected government officials of both races and sexes saw the Black community as approving (relatively speaking) the struggle for women's rights when that struggle is carried out by White women but disapproving when it is carried out by Black women (as was suggested from other evidence in Chapter 4). The White community, on the other hand, seems to have been viewed as lend-

ing support, albeit slight, to women who advocate woman's rights, whether these advocates were White or Black. The glaring exception to this latter generalization, of course, seems to have been the mass media, which
were thought to be like the Black community insofar as they rewarded
White female defenders of women's rights, while punishing Black female
defenders of those rights.

Further, Table 5.16 suggests the possibility that advocacy of birth
control (with its possible racial discrimination connotations, as discussed
in Chapter 4) may have been normatively more inappropriate for Black
women than for Black men, in the eyes of every constituency, and that
therefore those female officials who persisted in such advocacy were pe-
nalized with sharply reduced election help. Advocacy of health and day-
care centers, however, may have been judged more appropriate for women
than for men in the Black community. To give a highly speculative interpretation of these findings, we suggest that it is as though initiative in the
conception of children were still regarded, in both Black and White communities, as the prerogative of males—or as a nonmanipulable happen-
stance of "nature"—whereas once such conception has occurred, care for
the child becomes defined, at least in the Black community, as a definite
obligation of females.

Motivations

Turning to the bearing of officials' motivations on perceived election
help (Table 5.17), we find that among Black officials in both regions the
Black community was perceived as giving more election help to officials
who desired to correct social injustices, while the White community was

Table 5.17. Associations Between Motivations and Perceived Election Help
(Yule's Q)

| | South | | | | North | | | |
	Inside	Correct	Prestige	Serve	Inside	Correct	Prestige	Serve
				Black Officials				
BEH	—.01	.26	—.34	—.10	—.03	.29	.04	—.02
WEH	.25	—.35	—.30	—.27	.02	—.40	—.26	.05
PEH	—.24	.09	—.05	.34	—.17	—.26	.15	.12
MEH	.20	.25	—.33	—.31	.08	—.03	—.03	—.14
				White Officials				
BEH	.08	—.04	—.15	—.16	—.01	.32	.23	—.24
WEH	.11	—.01	.03	.05	.17	.14	.06	—.06
PEH	.35	.44	.34	—.45	—.08	.28	.08	—.23
MEH	.10	.18	.20	.00	.00	.08	.21	—.02

perceived as denying such officials election help. Although this difference is not borne out in the data on southern White officials, the direction of difference is borne out in the data on their northern White counterparts. Further, among Black officials, the media seem to have been perceived as more favorable toward those desiring to correct social injustices than were the political parties. However, among White officials this relationship seems to have been reversed.

Population Size and Percent Black

If we now examine the bearing of ideologies on perceived election help when population size and percent Black are held constant, we should gain some important and detailed information. For example, we can find out such things as whether integrationism was an asset with respect to perceived election help from large Black communities in southern, more urban areas, or whether liberalism was an asset with respect to help from the mass media in more rural areas outside the South. But before approaching such detailed questions—and in order to approach them best— it will be useful to examine the bearing simply of population size and of percent Black on the distribution of perceived election help.

Table 5.18 indicates that with three minor exceptions all types of perceived election help varied directly with population size. This finding may be taken as some overall validation of our indexes of election help since, all other things being equal, one would expect reports of greater help where the sources of help were greater.

Table 5.18. Percent High Perceived Election Help, Holding Constant Population Size and Percent Black

	South Population Size				North Population Size			
	Small		Large		Small		Large	
	Percent Black				Percent Black			
	Low	High	Low	High	Low	High	Low	High
				Black Officials				
BEH	47	35	71	58	33	30	44	33
WEH	51	27	65	42	77	33	75	39
PEH	40	33	53	39	44	44	59	42
MEH	51 (70)	33 (138)	78 (51)	55 (31)	53 (75)	41 (99)	62 (149)	55 (64)
				White Officials				
BEH	33	52	50	47	17	32	42	48
WEH	76	60	80	74	53	42	56	50
PEH	52	44	75	74	53	39	90	67
MEH	48 (21)	21 (85)	65 (20)	49 (49)	34 (53)	29 (31)	64 (62)	44 (46)

Turning now to the interregional comparisons provided by this table, note that in all population-size-by-percent-Black categories, southern Black officials reported more help from the Black community and (with one minor exception) less help from the White community than did their Black counterparts outside the South. Further, southern Black officials consistently reported less help from their party apparatuses, but there were no clear or consistent regional differences in perceived help from the mass media. It does not seem unreasonable to speculate that these tendencies may have been consequences of racially more segregated political traditions and of historically closer dependency of party apparatuses upon the White community inside than outside the South. The media apparatus, being partly of newer origins than the party apparatus and disposed to react to the unusual—whether "sensational" or merely "newsworthy"— seems not to have reflected these regional differences in election help presumably given to Black officials. One official whom we interviewed said:

> Interestingly enough, one person of a different race or color has an opportunity to get his views disseminated very generously by the news media because he is that one person, and the news media have given my views very broad coverage for that fact alone. The great majority on the council take a second thought before voting me down on certain pertinent issues lest they be tagged as bigots or racists or that sort of thing. Even the bigot or the racist—he doesn't like to have it known that he is.

The regional differences in White officials' perceptions of election help from the party and media apparatuses are not very different from the corresponding perceptions by Black officials. But a rather clear divergence does appear when we compare White and Black respondents' regional differences on perceived help from the Black and White communities. As pointed out in connection with Table 5.2, both Black and White officials were apt to view their own-race communities as helping more inside than outside the South, but White officials viewed their other-race community as helping more inside than outside the South, while Black officials viewed their other-race community as helping less inside and more outside the South. Table 5.17 adds to this the finding that the difference between the Black support received by White officials inside and outside the South was greatest in the more rural areas, less in the more urban areas, and least of all in the more urban areas of high percent Black.

There is another finding in Table 5.18 that should not be overlooked: Among Black officials, in both regions and in the more rural as well as the more urban election areas, more election help was reported from the Black community in areas of low percent Black than in areas of high percent

Black. That more election help should also be reported from the White community, the parties, and the media in such areas is readily understandable once it is realized that a relatively low percent Black implies a relatively high percent White. Then, to the extent that the White community, the political parties, and the mass media are all parts of the White "establishment," it makes sense that each such part should give (and be perceived as giving) greater help where it had more help to give, i.e., outside the larger Black communities, in areas of low percent Black and high percent White. What is anomalous, however, is that Black officials perceived the Black community as giving them more help where it had relatively less help to give or, alternatively, less help where it had relatively more help to give. This finding becomes all the more striking when the contrast with White officials is noted. With one minor exception, the latter reported more help from the Black community where the Black community was relatively large (high percent Black) than where it was relatively small.

Campbell et al. (noted in Wilson, 1966) reported survey findings that parallel these and give us what we believe is for the most part a reasonable explanation. They observe that "Negroes living in counties with a smaller proportion of Negroes in the population vote more often than do other Negroes living in counties with larger Negro populations" (1960:279). Campbell and his associates then offer but do not empirically support the explanation that "[w]here white dominance is numerically more extreme, there is apparently less community resistance to Negro voting . . . [and] . . . it is the informal, extralegal barriers—not state legislation—that account for much of the variability in the turnout of the Southern Negro" (1960:279, 281). Matthews and Prothro reached a similar empirical conclusion: "Negro registration in southern counties goes down as the proportion of Negroes goes up regardless of the other characteristics of the counties" (1963:20). And they also offered a similar (and similarly unsupported) explanation, "the larger the proportion of Negroes in an area, the more intense the vague fears of Negro domination that seem to beset southern whites" (1963:28).

We believe that our own findings not only confirm but elaborate on the findings and explanations of Campbell et al., and Matthews and Prothro. Thus Table 5.18 confirms that the Black community was perceived by Black officials to have given them more election help in the areas where Campbell et al., and Matthews and Prothro predict Black voters' fear of White hostility would be lower (i.e., where the percent Black was low). But our data elaborate on this with evidence that White hostility was perceived to be lower in low percent Black areas, insofar as Black officials reported more election help from the White community, and from their parties and the media as well, in these areas.

Now let us see how the perceptions of White officials varied with percent Black. Table 5.18 indicates that, in contrast with Black officials, White officials generally reported more election help from the Black community in areas of high percent Black. A simple extension of the Campbell et al., and Matthews-Prothro hypothesis can also account for this finding by suggesting that the same fear of White reprisals that reduced the election help given by the Black community to Black officials also increased the help that community gave to White officials. Note that White officials shared Black officials' opinions that more election help was received from the White community (and from the party and the media) in areas of low percent Black. (In the case of White officials, it seems more appropriate to refer to these areas as high percent White.)

Not only do our data add something to the finding that amount of Black political participation varies inversely with percent Black, they also permit some inferences about the ideological quality of that participation. We can, in short, find out the attitudes held by officials who reported receiving election help from Black communities of different relative sizes and then infer the dispositions of communities likely to have supported them. Accordingly, in Table 5.19 we show the bearing of Black indepen-

Table 5.19. Percent High Perceived Election Help, by Population Size, Percent Black, and Black Independence-Integrationism[a]

	Black Officials							
	South				North			
	Population Size				Population Size			
	Small		Large		Small		Large	
	Percent Black				Percent Black			
	Low	High	Low	High	Low	High	Low	High
BEH								
Independence	46	34	81	53	31	30	58	31
Integrationism	49	36	62	67	36	32	36	37
WEH								
Independence	46	22	69	26	66	30	75	31
Integrationism	57	34	62	67	87	40	76	48
PEH								
Independence	33	36	62	32	43	36	44	25
Integrationism	46	28	46	50	44	58	69	63
MEH								
Independence	54	33	85	53	51	46	59	47
Integrationism	49	32	71	58	56	34	64	63

[a] The smallest percentage base here is 12; the largest is 90. The first cell indicates that 46 percent of southern Black officials who represented election districts of small population size and low percent Black, and who also favored Black independence, perceived high BEH.

dence-versus-integration ideology on perceived election help, when population size and percent Black are simultaneously controlled. This table suggests that in the more urban (i.e., large population size) areas of low percent Black, advocates of Black independence reported more election help from the Black communities of both regions than did integrationists; in all other areas, integrationists reported more help from the Black communities. Thus not only the quantity, but also the quality of Black political participation seems to have been related to the relative size of the Black population.

Our data suggest, then, that when the Black community is small enough in relative size (i.e., percent Black, relative to the surrounding White community) and at the same time large enough in absolute size (i.e., population size, compared with other Black communities) two things may happen: (1) The Black community escapes the worst political intimidations of the White community and therefore participates more fully in the political process, but (2) feeling itself able to express its long-standing resentment of White domination more freely, it seizes this opportunity to support radical rejection of the White community rather than merger with it. Thus the evidence seems to point to the hypothesis that the Black community can become transformed from a minority that contests with the majority within a framework of allegiance to common rules to one that actively opposes, counters, and rejects the majority and its rules when that Black community (1) exceeds a certain minimum *absolute* population size and (2) also falls below a certain maximum *relative* population size (i.e., relative to the adjacent majority community).

Finally, it seems worth adding to all this the observation that the distribution of Black officials according to their views on Black independence and integration did not always correspond to the distribution of their self-reported success in getting election help from the Black community. This may be seen by comparing Table 3.18 with Table 5.19. Note, for example, that the demographic circumstance in which Black officials who supported Black independence said they received more help from the Black community than did integrationists (i.e., relatively small urban communities) was not the circumstance in which the former were most heavily concentrated either inside or outside the South. The same kind of discrepancy was true of integrationists.

Thus, if we assume that officials' perceptions of election help from the Black community were accurate, then neither Black independent nor integrationist officials seem to have capitalized on their potential election help, because they were generally underrepresented in areas where that potential seems to have been high and overrepresented in areas where that potential seems to have been low. But more broadly our data may reflect, by implication, the strategic problems that politicians and their parties face in deciding whether (1) to swim against the present tide of public opinion in expectation of, or in deliberate construction of, a future turning point; (2) to swim with the present tide, deliberately forestalling or negating a future turning point; or (3) to ride both the tide and the turns—thus literally "representing" their constituencies.

CHAPTER 6

Perceived Impact and Expected Future

Against the background of four chapters of chiefly statistical analysis of data from written questionnaires—questionnaires wherein responses were limited by standardized, fixed choices—we want now to give Black elected officials a chance to speak more freely for themselves, and the reader a chance to sample the flavor of their thoughts regarding their past accomplishments and future expectations. Therefore this chapter will be devoted entirely to a presentation and analysis of quotations on these issues from interviews with 34 Black elected officials.

Impact on the Black Community

One major impact that our respondents thought their elections had had was to develop within the Black community confidence in politics and government as potential instruments of Black progress[1]:

> I was first elected to office in 1960. As you know, Blacks are a small minority in my city. So after I was elected, it gave the Black community a certain amount of confidence in themselves. They had no confidence before that they could gain anything in the political as-

---

[1] Some indication that such confidence was not actually developed as fully as our respondents hoped may be found in Arthur Miller, Thad Brown, and Alden Raine, "Social Conflict and Political Estrangement, 1958–1972," 1973. Miller et al. report a general deterioration in trust in government between 1968 and 1972 with Blacks' trust deteriorating four times as fast as Whites'.

137

pects in the city. So, this gives them some confidence, but I had to prove myself to them, too, because we've been "sold down the river" so much that the Black people had no confidence in a Black elected official. So I had to prove myself. After I had proven myself to them, they have a lot more confidence now.

Q: Would you say that also carries over to the general political process—that they seek greater hope through the political process?

A: Oh, yes! They do, because they feel they have something now to vote for. In other words, they used to feel: "Well, it doesn't do me any good to vote, because they're going to do what they want anyway." But the Black community doesn't feel that way anymore, because they have something now to vote for.

*

I think the difference it has made to the Black community has been to give the Black community a feeling of belonging. They feel that they have a listening ear when they want to go to the city for a solution to a problem, or the righting of some wrong, or changing about of some inequity that has happened to them as a result of city forces. I think it's that they feel like the City Hall belongs to them too, because they see the Black image there, and they identify with it.

*

In a sense I've radicalized the political process for both communities by trying to relate the nature of politics to the life of the average person, which generally in this country is not a fully developed concept among either Black or White citizens, especially among Blacks, who being oppressed and discriminated against, have a tendency to feel that the government is usually their enemy, which to some extent is a very logical conclusion to arrive at.

*

Since we've got five Black judges, the policeman who goes out there and beats some Black person's head does not know but he may have to stand before one of those five Black judges. So, he's a little more circumspect now.

*

It makes White people dependent upon the decisions that are being made by Black people. This helps our thinking. This helps the thinking of our children in the future. The things that they are enjoying today were made possible by Black people.

The second impact informants reported was on the number of Blacks actually employed in government jobs.

> When I went into office in 1961, there were but three Black people in City Hall earning under $3,000 a year. Now in my city, 43 percent of the people who work in City Hall are Black and 50 percent of the directors who run my city are Black. At the time when I first went in, we had one councilman, myself. I, subsequently, appointed another one. There are now two Blacks and five Whites.

*

> I was able to change a Public Works Department which had two Black employees to one that now has over 70 percent Black employees. And in the Police Department, they're increasing Blacks again.

*

> My biggest problem going into office I think was with our uniformed divisions, like our Police and Fire departments. Our Fire Department has, with the exception of the last 18 months, been lily-white. This has been changed, and we're still far from being satisfied. It's also my goal to have every board, and there are 37, have minority representation so that we can have this input.

But despite the new faith in politics and government that they claimed to have engendered, and despite the increased governmental employment of Blacks that they fostered, informants were nearly unanimous in identifying a continuing lack of participation in government as the main shortcoming of the Black community.

> The leaders that we have followed have always been the leaders forced upon us by White people. They've been maintained by White people, and they serve White people. They keep the niggers quiet, and that's been their major role. They haven't dealt with the problems that affected Black people. Black people who run our schools run them as badly as do the White people who run them, because they are not answerable to the Black communities for how they educate our kids; they're answerable to the White community. It's a White man who keeps them in their jobs. Until Blacks are responsible to Blacks, then we are going to just continue that way.

*

> I think that Blacks have to learn that once you've elected a person, your job isn't finished. Often we feel, you know, that we elected John Doe, so we don't have to worry anymore. Just tell him our problems. But there's a need for political pressures at times. There is a need for

the community to actively support an issue by whatever means they decide. I feel that we don't have enough of this in the Black community. Now, the Whites are able to do this. They have the resources. If they don't want to come themselves, they have lobbyists to protect their interests.

Q: Blacks don't take it upon themselves to come to the state capital, do they?

A: No, they don't unless it's a crucial time. Now, if the schools are in trouble, they'll come up here in droves. If the ADC mothers want an increase, they'll come up here on buses. But what I'm talking about is consistency in the process and making it work. And this calls for a little time and endurance, and I don't think we've gotten to that point yet.

*

My greatest need as an elected official is that I feel that I should have more backing than I have, because we can get down on the streets and someone will say: "Why hasn't this been done; when are we going to get this done, or when are we going to get so and so and so and so?" But I feel they need to be right up there before the City Council supporting you on these issues. I talked with many, many other Blacks and they have the same thoughts I have: that the Negro will get out in the street but don't give you the backing that you should have. But when it comes time to vote, they'll vote for you. As many Blacks as possible should, every time the City Council chambers open, attend City Council meetings and support the issue.

One judge, in particular, also stressed his own responsibility for keeping the Black community informed.

In the Black community it's a matter of keeping faith and keeping their confidence because to the extent that I and other Black officials can keep their confidence and their faith, we also keep their faith and confidence in the system itself. And when I say system, let me hasten to define. I'm talking about our constitutional system. I'm talking about the system of government set forth in the constitution. I'm not talking about our economic system. I'm not talking about our social system. That means then that what you do has got to always make sense to them, which means they have to be informed of why you do what you do. Why it is you have to do what it is you do. If they don't like it, they also have to be taught how they can go about changing it. But until it's changed, you have to follow it.

This official went on to point out the reciprocity that is involved.

You've got what really amounts to a circle. Black judges will stick their necks out more if they are assured of sufficient Black support in the community. On the other hand, the Black community is going to give more support to the judge who sticks his neck out. Somewhere along the line somebody has to exhibit confidence in somebody else.

Some informants explicitly emphasized their desire for a more sophisticated quality, as well as a greater quantity, of participation.

The most important thing is to increase the knowledge of the Black population regarding the roles of government at all levels. Because without knowing it is impossible for them to put the heat where it needs to be put.

*

Some of my constituents, and I'm speaking of the Blacks, feel a councilman's job is only to fix streets, to solve a personal problem— some dilemma they might be in, fix street lights, stop police brutality, and so, it's kind of hard to relate and explain your position and go about fulfilling your obligation as a councilman.

*

I have a file of over 25,000 people that I have seen since 1961 and helped them. Now, this means a lot to Blacks—that you help them get jobs and internal affairs and their personal affairs. But this is really not the thing. They overlook what has really been done for the entire city that will give their children an opportunity to participate in a society that they never could be a part of. And this is the type of educational process that must be placed among us, not "that councilman is okay. He put me on my job, or he got me put back in my home, or he got me a home, or he got me out of jail." This is what they call a good councilman. But a man who could sit down and plan and know the interworkings of government, plan for the specific needs of the community and for posterity: this is a councilman to me. I require every one of my councilmen to have taken courses in urban affairs and urban studies. I mean it's most important. You know, a lot of the Whites didn't like it, and thought that I was interfering with the fact that they thought they had enough educational background. I said, "This is not the point." I said, "The times are changing. Young people are saying a great many things that a great many of us don't understand, and we've got to learn how to communicate with them in order to write the proper legislation to get the job done."

*

An intensive program of education of Black people, Black voters, Black constituency with the cooperation, of course, of the Black elected official for that particular area should be done. But there is a great deal of misunderstanding and apprehension. For instance, I probably get as many calls about city problems as the aldermen do. They just don't understand that I am a member of the state legislature. However, I go right ahead and I call about garbage collection, I write letters about the street lights that need to be put in this place and that place, or four-way stop signs, or a street may need resurfacing. I go right ahead and do this, because this is some little service that you can perform when you are not able to do anything else.

Those few who felt that they had adequate participation and support from their Black constituencies seemed gratified indeed.

I think the biggest aid in the Black community is being able to assemble readily the leaders of the Black community on any problem or any areas or topics that may affect the Black community only. Another thing that I initiated is that I try every six months to have a Black caucus for the city not only for the leaders of the community, but for the people who would like to come and ask any questions as to what's going on in City Hall.

*

One of the things that I've done which I believe is unique since I've been elected is to hold an annual legislative conference to which I attempt to attract as many and as cross-sectional a group of people in my district as possible—one all-day conference that's roughly divided into two parts: first, morning sessions are known as "Reports to the People," at which I attempt to report on what I've been doing. It's an accountability type of thing. I've done this in conjunction with state representatives whose districts are often a part of my own. We have jointly, over the past seven years now, had these annual legislative conferences. We have taken many of the recommendations from the citizens gathered there and have actually executed them as law, as bills. Some of the bills have passed as law.

Q: So the communication and the feedback have been effective?

A: I think so. I think it is probably the annual highlight of my legislative career. It's a chance for me to report back, to be responsive. At the same time receive feedback. And we not only concern ourselves with legislative recommendations. We recognize our limitations here. We also recognize that all of the problems that face people in my community cannot be solved by legislation. So, we also engage in community action.

*

My greatest help has been the support I get from the Black community. I've attempted to keep the lines open and make my activities known to my constituency. Therefore, I'm very seldom bothered by some of the attacks.

*

I have a tremendous hangup about community participation. But at the same time, I have the courage to tell Blacks who misunderstand the concept of the federal government and the state government that community participation does not mean community takeover. And this understanding in a great many urban cities has caused public officials to refrain from using, and even listening to, the community—which they must do. You must know what people want before you can provide it for them, and you've got to have this rapport with the community. Now, I have no problem with them, because I'm with them constantly—born in the ghetto, raised in the ghetto, and I still live in the ghetto, and I don't ever intend to leave. I can afford to leave, but I don't think I could do an effective job for my people.

Still, closeness to one's constituency had its price.

I wouldn't change it, and I don't regret it but I have a longing desire for anonymity sometimes. My telephone is listed and I am therefore never out of the eye of the public and never away from the demands of the public. I am there to serve the people I represent, but 24 hours a day? And, of course, the answer to that has to be "no" because then one's family life begins to suffer and that is critically important.

Impact on the White Community

We have indicated that the main difference that interviewed Black officials reported having made to the Black community was to engender confidence in the American political and governmental *system*. By contrast, the primary reported effect on the White community was to engender confidence in (or allay fears about) *themselves*, both personally and as representatives of Black people generally.

Well, my big problem in the White community was that I was Black, and they feared me. They did not know whether I would do the same kind of things to White folks that White folks had been doing to Black folks all these years. But I have shown a propensity to be fair, which in some cases surprised many White folks, and gradually I began to win them.

*

Before this, White people had never seen a Black person elected to office and they didn't know what he could do, and they were the victims of their fears and prejudices. Now that they've seen some Black people in government, they know that Black people can deal with issues that confront them adequately and in a manner which in some ways serves aspirations of the middle group of White folk and the poor even more that some White councilmen had.

*

I've come to the position that the Whites understand my stance personally. But I don't think that this can be applied to another Black man. I think we're still at the point that each one of us has to go through these gyrations one at a time until a larger number of us prove a point, so we won't have to review it anymore.

*

The White people actually put me in office the first time, because they felt if I could do something to help the Black people, I could do something to help them. They saw that in the district which I represent the White councilman was not doing anything to help the White community in that district. He couldn't get anything done. He wasn't trying. When I was elected, I started programs in the district, and the things that he couldn't get out, I began to get the wheels turning to get them done. So, the White people have been on my side ever since.

*

With the White people, a great many times you find that you hear that I am doing more for Blacks than I am for Whites. But this is not hard to overcome, because I speak in the White communities and I tell them that someone has to bring the rest of the community up to standards. And I say, "I know and realize that every Black is not going to make it as every White is not going to make it, but the opportunity to participate in a free society must be there, and we must provide these tools and the vehicle for this. This is all we're trying to do."

All of our respondents expressed the belief that they had made a difference in some way—a significant difference and a difference for the better—for the Black community, for the White community, and often, for the entire political-governmental process in the United States. None seems to have taken government office perfunctorily and none viewed himself or herself as a helpless cog in an undeviating machine.

The Future They Foresee

Let us now examine our respondents' comments regarding the future (as seen in 1971) of political relations between the Black and White communities and of Black elected officials, after which we will report a few of our informants' general views of the entire national and international prospect.

The Future of Political Relations Between the Black and White Communities

Our informants foresaw three principal future tendencies: (1) a continued strengthening of Black political control of the cities; but (2) the political and financial weakening of the cities; and (3) the formation of political coalitions between the Black community and minorities within the White community to preserve and invigorate the cities.

In every major city throughout the United States, we have a larger number of Black people being elected to public office. It means virtually nothing; it means they are elected but have no power. Every fifth bill going through virtually every major legislature in the United States is taking the power away from the city-elected officials and putting it in the county or the state. And so, there they will be elected with virtually no money and nothing to support the inner-city but federal grants.

*

If the trend continues, the Whites moving to the suburbs and the Blacks moving to the city, and the governmental structure remaining as it is, I think that Blacks will be in control of most of the large cities within the next 15 years. However, the White power structure is now moving to a different place, because they realize that this will happen soon. It's only a matter of time. So they're moving now to regional government, you see. Regional government will mean that the people in the suburbs will share in the governing of that region. So, as we are about to seize cities, they move to a different kind of government.

*

Blacks are quite concerned now that we have the beginnings of substantial representation that this is going to be diluted. Now the reason for this is because we've had consistent exit to the suburbs, and so we do not have the population really to warrant the amount of representation that we have at this immediate time. We are in a bind as to how to keep the amount of representatives that we have. Now in the House there is a problem with getting out-state representatives to support any measures that are going to bring aid to the city primarily, because there is a concentration in the city of your poor and your Blacks, your elderly people who all need services which cost money. So, we must think in terms of trying to salvage as much of this representation as we can. And as long as we base it on population, minority groups are in trouble in terms of having the numbers to control this. We feel that our city is dying and our hands are tied as to what we can do to turn it around. We have urban renewal, which has removed much of the housing that was there, and that land is dormant. The rest of the land has gone into expressways so that our suburban friends can traverse back and forth to work. We have many people working in the city but no one really sustaining it.

*

So many Whites are moving into the suburban areas today, and this leaves the city broke. They come into the city; they use the city's transportation system. They use all the resources that the city has, and when evening comes, they go back out into the suburban areas.

Belief in the feasibility of future coalitions with parts of the White community seemed to be based on some past experience. Thus, speaking of a mayoral election, one informant said:

At best the Black registered voting strength was between 35 and 40 percent at the time of that election. So that means that obviously the remaining 60–65 percent of the vote was White. [The Black candidate] picked up 10 or 15 percent, which means he picked up anywhere from one out of six to one out of five White votes. This leads me to believe that there is some basis for coalition with some of the more advanced elements in the White community.

Two informants emphasized the bases for political coalitions.

I believe the basic problems of this country happen to be reflected most acutely in the Black experience. What are those problems? Housing. We are the ones who have the most acute housing problems. Many millions of Whites have it, and they're going to learn that in order to get housing for themselves, they're going to have to link up with our political base. The problem of helplessness—we happen to be twice the percentage of unemployed in any given community, and the Whites who are increasingly becoming unemployed are going to learn that their interests, that to serve their interests in getting jobs, they're going to have to link up with the political power of Blacks, and that's going to make race relations improve, I believe, over the decade of the seventies.

*

There's strength in numbers; and when you're able to put together a team of Blacks, Puerto Ricans, Indians, poor Whites, liberal Whites, all of whom in their own respective capacity are minorities, then you have the possibility of becoming the majority. And I think the future of achievement of Blacks in politics is through coalitions.

One official expressed belief in the persistence of racism among White voters, while another expressed optimism in this regard:

If you have a majority of White [people living in an area] and you have a White candidate running and a Black, I can't see in the foreseeable future when this ratio exists that you have the Black [candidate] prevailing no matter how good his qualifications are. A whole lot of Whites may feel that the Black is better qualified credentialwise, but somehow, when they pull the lever, there's some type of racism coming out.

*

I think that it does look promising. I think eventually this notion that Blacks will not only represent Blacks, but Whites, will gradually begin to take hold. One of the things we can't measure right now is the fact that the new levels of the struggle for liberation have an unconscious effect on the masses of White people that cannot be immediately translated into votes or tangible programs. But it's clear that many of the myths and stereotypes that have traditionally been used to rationalize the subjugation of Black people in this country are invalid to even the most unperceptive White person. There has to be a lead time before we finally overcome these racist notions. I think the psychological, the unconscious levels, are being deeply affected and that they will be manifested probably sooner than later if these masses of White people are not cynically manipulated by White political leadership.

Thus, although the prediction of increased Black political control of the cities is negated by the prediction that the cities will be politically and financially disabled, it seems fair to say that some of our informants were made mildly optimistic, on balance, by the prospect of coalitions with disadvantaged sectors of the White community.

The Future of Black Elected Officials

Our respondents were doubtful that a new national party would be formed by Blacks (with or without other minority group allies), but they did not reject that possibility entirely.

> I believe there is a need for one of the present parties, if it can be done, to change radically its position; and specifically, I think the one that probably would be more amenable to that change would be the Democratic party. It is my prediction that if that doesn't happen in the very near future, we are in fact going to see a nationwide Black and other minority coalition that will come together into a national party.

*

> I don't say that a Black party won't emerge, but at this point the battle is inside the Democratic party to use the tremendous leverage that we have. Twenty percent of all the votes that the presidential nominee on the Democratic ticket received in 1968 came from Black people, and that was even though only 58 percent of the eligible Blacks were registered; and only 42 percent of the eligible Blacks voted. This means that we have a power that can almost be doubled. Well, you can't take that outside to form a party that would take years to get when we can throw that into challenging the ancient racist powers that have operated as brokers within the Democratic party. And it's going eventually to even have an effect on the Republican party, which will have to move to the left to counter that. We have to skillfully construct a tactic that will move into the Republican party and force them, even against most of their wills, to make this change.

Most informants expected the number of Black elected officials to increase, and some also expected that increase to bring some unwelcome consequences.

> As we see more of us becoming elected to various bodies, we're also going to aspire individually to certain positions, and there certainly has to be competition. As a result of this competition, there's going

to be political maneuvering and political hostilities that will tend to divide us. I hope this won't come about in the next three or four years anyway, because we can't afford it.

*

Well, I think as we become more successful, we're going to become more divided. This ought not to be true. I think that it's a sad thing. The worse shape we're in, the closer we stick together. As times get better for us, the more we relax, the less concern we have for those of us under similar circumstances. This is not an unusual thing.

At least one official thought he perceived some dissension already.

Frankly, the Black Congressional Caucus, in my judgment, is concerned with themselves—the Black congressmen. I don't think they could care less what happens where there is one Black councilman fighting to try to get a job done. I think they'll fight to do something for Harlem, for instance, because you've got a tremendous vote there. They'll fight to do something for Newark because you've got a lot of votes there—Detroit, for instance, certain districts in Chicago, but I don't think the boys out in the boondocks stand a chance of getting their aid.

Some General Views and Forecasts

One official was outstanding for expressing a broad optimism about the future of this country and its people.

I think that I see and feel the inherent respect for other people's rights running generally through Americans of goodwill. Most Americans, I think, believe that all Americans are entitled to the rights and privileges as set forth in the Constitution, and as Americans, they should participate in the benefits of our society. When the people are put to this test, they demonstrate that they are on the side of right. I have yet to find masses of American people denying the basic rights to their fellow Americans. What is my impression and my experience is that a few individuals who are well organized are the ones who seek to deny other Americans their rights and frustrate the will of a majority of people who want to be decent and do the right things.

Most, such as the following three, however, expressed ambivalent expectations tending toward the pessimistic.

I think I have a restrained optimism at this point. The emerging Third World powers, the fact that there are other superpower nations in the world is going to finally have an inhibiting effect on this country. The international pressures on America are so great that she cannot persist in the kinds of ultra-conservative political acts that she might otherwise engage in. I think, though, there are some other issues that could lead me to have a guarded negative view of the future of this country. We're running out of land, air, energy, space—all the givens that have been exploited by the giant corporations. We're really running out of a livable earth. We're so busy fighting still over old myths of racism and class that we're now, for the most part, unaware of the fact that there are new challenges to the existence of mankind as a civilization on the earth.

*

I think that America today is at a real crossroads. We've known, certainly since 1967 when the major explosions occurred in our ghettos across the nation, that grievous social injustices lie at the root of the cynicism, the resentment that characterizes the Black community. The Kerner Commission pointed out that massive sums— reparations, if you want to call it that—would have to be spent to correct the social conditions symbolized by these explosions or the racist polarization will continue and intensify. I think you know as well as I that nothing substantial has been done to correct these situations. . . . It is not accidental that as Black people in city after city are moving to achieve political power, the Police Department of this city should declare its independence and superiority or should actively enter the political arena. Now, it's my contention that no military force has any business engaging in politics. But I foresee military dictatorship rising in our cities as a result of corrupt, racist, and largely White police departments. So that when Black people should achieve political control of the cities, they will be actually held in chancery by their own police departments. And when you combine this with the army's plans for suppressing future riots with detention centers that we know already exist, then you begin to get some picture of the type of repression that is developing. . . . It's my opinion that this country is at the crossroads, that it may explode and destroy itself. I am under no illusions that the Black population which is 10 percent can in a confrontation defeat the White population which is 90 percent and has all the tools. We can't win. . . . . [But] I also say this, that those White racists who believe the solution to the problem in America can be along Hitler's lines—that the Blacks can be wiped out in the same manner as the Jews were in Nazi Germany—also suffer an illusion. It is possible for the overwhelming strength of the White population and the White power structure to destroy the Black population. But the struggle would be so bloody that America, in the course of that destruction, would itself be destroyed.

*

I see the system of capitalism which we have as requiring a certain number of rejects. The capitalist system is a system that involves competition, and anytime you have competition, there have to be some losers. Historically, this has always been true in America. All of the ethnic groups that have come here have paid their time in being the losers at the bottom rung and have gradually assimilated into the culture and are no longer at the bottom proportionate to their numbers. I'm quite sure there are some poor Italians, but they are relatively few at this time. Now with Black people who were the last to come up—and we got to that bottom rung after ceasing to be property—we haven't really gone too far, and there's nobody to take our place at the bottom rung. I do not see a time when the pattern would be reversed to the point that our proportion of the poor, of the unemployed, would be the same as our proportion to the population. The people of the Republic of New Africa, of course, give one answer—a separate state. I do not see that as a viable solution due to the fact that we would be surrounded by very powerful nations, and we would continue to be dependent upon their actions even though we're in a completely separate state. If this separate state moved in any way that the large country did not want it to, it could be done away with quite easily. Pan-Africanism—I cannot very readily see it as an out. In my acquaintances with brothers and sisters from the mother land, I have found that they would be quite willing, say for example, to accept you into their country. They would most likely accept me into their country, but then what happens to my grandmother and my two aunts who are on welfare? They do not want liabilities. So the other people who are left here would be left to the dogs, so to speak. I'm not blaming the countries of Africa for not being able to say that they will take everybody, because they are just building their nations, and it would be disastrous for them to attempt to accept all of us. So, I'm not negating it all, but I'm saying for Black people to say, perhaps, to build up Africa is forgetting the 90 percent of the people who live here in America. So as for the future, I just don't see any answer.

Q: None at all? Then it looks pretty bleak for you?

A: Yes. It does to me. I would say that at the present time it appears to me that Black people are dispensable for the most part. At one time, before the industrial development that we have now, we were needed to do something. At the present time, we are not that needed. When I say "we," I'm speaking in terms of the masses. The laboring man is no longer needed. And I don't know. I don't see necessarily that they will go around shooting Black people, but if insurrections continue or get started again, I would certainly see the possibility of a great catastrophe. I don't know that this will happen, but I don't see any positive paths. About the only thing positive is when you go to the international level, realizing that the majority of the peoples of the world are non-White. And this, of course, can have many results from the standpoint of the international focal point. But on a national focal point here in this nation, divorced from all the rest of this, I don't see very much hope. Some people ask me, Why do you mess around with it? I mess around with it for a pretty basic reason. I think whatever comes, whether it be good or whether it be bad, don't just sit and say there's no use in doing anything: *do*. Do whatever there is that can be done that makes the existence of people more bearable.

Q: Do you see any positive signs from among Black elected officials on the national level? Do you see any signs there in the White administration or anything like that? Any sensitivity to these types of issues to which you are speaking?

A: I see sensitivity, but then when you measure things in terms of actions, which I like to do too, I don't see that much. For example, the revenue sharing thing is a disaster. I am quite convinced that when the direction of spending is determined at a more local level it will become very much a political thing on that local basis. Therefore, these funds will be used by the politicians to satisfy most of the people and get votes. Since the places where Black people control on a local basis are very limited, satisfying most of the people means satisfying White people in most instances. Therefore, the revenue sharing program, if it becomes a reality, will again deal Black communities out. There's a lot of liberal talk in most places where you get together with White politicians. But though not all of them realize what an action like this means, most of them, I'm quite sure, do realize what it means basically. It means that this is a way for us to give the people something, and we give the people something in order to stay in office.

Q: In a similar vein, what do you see as the future of this country domestically and internationally?

A: Domestically, the future of the country depends, as I see it, on the various groups who are the dissenters from the status quo, young people, Third World people, Black people. Maybe this dissent is something that will pass from the young White radical. I go to school with them, and I listen to them, and they make me sound like the most conservative person in the world sometimes. But I wonder. They tell me that back in the 1960s they were just as radical. Many of them now are sitting in the $30,000 jobs calling the shots, and the shots that they are calling are not radical. So, the things the kids are saying in the 1970s, they said in the 1960s, and might have said in the 1950s. I don't know.

Q: But the Blacks don't have as many options of that type, I gather?

A: The Black will stay back. He's locked in. The young, White radical is not locked in and can make choices. So, if the White radicals did remain fairly radical as they get older and attain a position of power, if coalitions could be formed between the dissident groups provided they remained dissident, then there would be some prospect for the country. A lot depends on the positions that the young men and women in the universities, who are in their 20s now, take ten years hence.

Q: Well, how does the situation look internationally? Do you see them as tied together or what?

A: Internationally, I would say that the situation looks much better. I'd say that the example set by China, the strong fight of the people of Vietnam against overpowering obstacles, releases Third World, Black people from the myth of the White man's absolute superiority. When you have a country like China that can raise itself to such a significant level in a number of years, it crushes the whole idea that nothing can be accomplished except by the White man's way. When you have a people who defy being put down consistently with all the weapons that America has, it says that maybe he is not invincible. The mere fact that the developing countries are proceeding at such a rate means that in a matter of time the balance of power in the world will change. So, I think that the only thing that will change America, unless the other coalitions that I mentioned do remain steady, will be outside pressures. When White America realizes that they are a minority in the world, and that the majority of the people have achieved a strength that is threatening to them, which we have not achieved at this point, then I feel America must change.

CHAPTER 7 □□
Conclusion

At least three sets of related findings and speculations deserve a last look here. They bear upon (1) Black officials' ideological attitudes; (2) their perceptions of electoral constituencies; and (3) their perspectives on the future.

Although the proponents of several ideological attitudes were examined in this study, three varieties seem especially interesting: those who supported Black independence, those who supported socioeconomic liberalism, and those who supported equality for women. It seems important to emphasize that among Black officials these three viewpoints were not strongly intercorrelated: Liberalism and support for Black independence were only weakly correlated, but support for Black independence and feminism were negatively and weakly correlated. Thus our study emphasized how easily a Black official could tend to be a racial "radical" without being a socioeconomic "radical," and how easily he or she could be either without being a gender "radical."

The low level of interrelationships among these viewpoints seems partly accounted for by the finding that personal background factors were often related to them in different ways. For example, education was related positively to liberalism, somewhat less positively to feminism, but it was unrelated to support for Black independence. And although those who tended toward any of these "radical" viewpoints reported their party affiliation as "Other" more often than either Democratic or Republican, Black independents and liberals were more prevalent among Black Democrats

155

than among Black Republicans, and feminists seem to have rejected both
of the latter affiliations. The three viewpoints were also somewhat vari-
ably associated with different types of office: Legislative-executive officials at the state level were more liberal and more feminist (though not
more favorable to Black independence) than those at county and city
levels. Law enforcement and educational officials, however, did not noticeably differ from level to level in any of these regards.

The three viewpoints seem to have had different influences on the
election help that Black officials received. Such officials generally reported
receiving more election help from the Black community if they were
liberals than if they were proponents of Black independence, and the
least if they were feminists. In this latter connection, we found that although Black males gained some election help from their constituencies
if they were feminists, Black female feminists seem to have sustained
severe losses of election help. Thus, ironically, even the advocacy of
women's rights seems to have been a prerogative of men more than of
women.

However, the three viewpoints did share features in common—
either partly or wholly—and one of these was a stronger link to direct-
action than to more conventional forms of social action. This is not surprising when one considers that Black independence, liberalism, and
feminism all run counter to present-day conventional American values
and, given such powerful opposition, they are apt to be seen as calling for
uncommonly vigorous means to fulfill them. In our judgment, it is precisely this linkage of unconventional means to unconventional goals that
most deserves the term "militancy," and our data suggest that according
to this criterion Black independence "radicals" were considerably more
militant than political "radicals" or gender "radicals." We offered one
speculative explanation for the greater militancy of proponents of Black
independence (in addition to their apparent unpopularity): Black racism,
the ideological converse of White racism (i.e. Black supremacist hereditarianism as contrasted with White supremacist hereditarianism), may
have had some currency among Black officials and, if so, would have given
special impetus and daring to those who promoted Black independence.

Racial hereditarianism in general, whether favoring Whites or Blacks,
carried somewhat mixed relationships to the three viewpoints in question. It was negatively associated with political liberalism and feminism
(especially the former) among officials of both racial identities, but it was
positively (though not strongly) associated with support for Black independence among Black officials. Moreover, hereditarianism clearly played
a more central role in the ideology systems of White officials than in those
of Black officials, and the former seemed to be moderately rewarded for

such beliefs. Thus White officials, in the North as well as in the South, reported receiving more election help from the White community if they believed in racial hereditarianism than if they did not, but Black officials generally reported that this belief made no difference in election help from either the Black or the White communities.

Black and White officials also differed sharply in their motivations for seeking elected government office. Among Black officials the desire to correct social injustices was given high priority, and low priority was given to serving the country, while among White officials these desires received just the reverse priorities. Our analysis has suggested that Black officials tended to draw more social distinctions among Americans—for example, between the beneficiaries and the victims of social injustices and between those who are "on the inside" and those who are "on the outside." White officials, on the other hand, seemed much more prone to see the United States as "one nation, indivisible," and—considering the strong connection between their desire to serve the country and their belief in racial hereditarianism—they may have tended to add "indivisibly White, with liberty and justice for Whites first."

However, despite these inferred differences in perceptions and despite the differences directly shown in our data regarding motivations for seeking public office, a general similarity prevailed across both races in the direction of associations between these motivations and liberalism, feminism, and support for Black independence. Thus, generally speaking, we found positive associations between the desire to correct social injustices and all three of these viewpoints, but negative associations between them and the desire to serve the country.

It therefore seems fair to say that support for Black independence, liberalism, and feminism were complex ideological viewpoints that carried both similar and dissimilar implications for the officials who adopted them. In this sense, our findings seem to point out how misleading an unqualified "radical" label may be.

Such data on officials' ideologies and motivations for seeking office tell us something about how these respondents thought of themselves (e.g., as favoring Black independence or integration, political liberalism or conservatism, etc.). But data on their perceptions of sources of their election support tell us something about how they thought of their constituencies (e.g., as "helpful" or "hindering"). Perhaps the most interesting finding in this regard concerns the demographic conditions under which maximum election help was reported from the Black community. Consonant with other studies, we found that Black officials reported more election help from the Black community when that community was small relative to the White community than when it was large. But contrary to the implication of at least one other study, we found that Black officials reported more help from the larger, urban, Black communities than from the smaller, more rural, ones—that is, more help when the Black community was large relative to other Black communities than when it was small. To these findings we then added some information about the ideologies of Black officials who were supported by the different types of Black communities. In this way, we were led to the general speculation that a Black community may increase the amount of its political participation and also change the quality of that participation from favoring Black officials who support integration to favoring those who support independence, when it passes above some threshold of absolute size and also is below some threshold of size relative to the surrounding White community. Such a Black community may develop intense feelings of being oppressed and, at the same time, a strong sense of its own strength and capability. Together, these sentiments may result in a high degree of frustration followed by aggressive secessionism.

Regarding the different impact that Black officials thought they had on the Black community and on the White community, whatever their sizes, the officials we interviewed emphasized a different impact for each community. They stressed their impact on the Black community's confidence in the American political and governmental system, but they stressed their impact on the White community's confidence in Black officials themselves, both personally and as representatives of other Black people. One can imagine this difference arising partly from prior differences in officials' assessment of each community's political capacities. That is, even before their entry into politics, Black respondents could conceivably have thought of the Black community as lacking mainly in trust of the political-governmental system as a means toward Black progress, and the White community may have been judged lacking mainly in trust of Blacks as competent and fair-minded officers of government. Officials who thought like this would be expected to pay close attention to their progress along these lines. In this connection, it is noteworthy that Black officials did not seem very interested in getting into office and then "running things" from the inside with no "outside interference." On the contrary, they actively sought and fostered such "interference." Perhaps only officials who had a great desire to instill public confidence in the system and in themselves and great confidence in their ability to withstand public scrutiny of their activities, could so urgently seek to extend public participation in these activities. And it should not go unnoticed that some years ago one might not have been surprised to see lack of trust in Black officials attributed to the Black as well as to the White community. It may therefore be highly significant that no such attribution was made in any of our interviews. These Black officials seem largely to have taken personal trust from the Black community for granted—a sign, perhaps, of increasing Black solidarity.

Neither that welcome possibility nor any other, however, seems to have relieved our interviewees at least of a fundamental pessimism regarding the future. Clearly, Black elected officials wanted to improve the lot of Black Americans generally, and still more generally, to strengthen American democracy for all minorities; the increased political participation that they sought was designed to strengthen their hands to this end. But the same Black officials also knew that American cities were threatened by the majority-White exodus of population and finances, followed by efforts to reduce the political power of the remaining Black and minority-White inhabitants. Thus the future that these Black officials foresaw seems reducible to the still unanswered question of whether political power wielded by Blacks and other minorities in the cities can grow quickly enough to catch and reverse the urban exodus of economic and political power, forestall any intensification of racist reaction, and thus reconstruct the cities and, hopefully, the nation as well.

There can be little question that the Black community, during the past ten years, has come to wield greater direct power than ever before in the political and governmental life of the United States. The higher levels of Black voter participation, and the election of a greater number of Blacks to government office are not only principal components of that achievement but principal guarantors of its continuation. But it is undeniable that, despite these advances, equity between the levels of power residing in the Black community and in the White community is still nowhere in sight. Any second Reconstruction that recent Black political gains may conceivably herald is therefore not nearly developed enough (and especially not strongly enough supported by equity in higher levels of American economic life) to resist blows such as crushed the first Reconstruction. And if these blows do in fact materialize, if the Black community is driven back from even the slight political gains of the recent past, or prevented from deepening and extending them, that tragedy would engulf more than the Black community alone. Given the scope of social structural and attitudinal bases on which these gains rest and from which the Black community moves forward, the many ramifications of such an attack would gravely endanger representative government for all Americans— White, as well as Black.

For these reasons, the rapid achievement of political, economic, and social equity between the Black and the White communities and of equality between Black and White individuals remains an indispensable defense of American democracy.

References

Campbell, Angus, *White Attitudes Toward Black People,* Ann Arbor, Mich.: Institute for Social Research, University of Michigan, 1971.

Campbell, Angus, Philip E. Converse, Warren E. Miller, Donald E. Stokes, *The American Voter,* New York: John Wiley, 1960.

Campbell, David and Joe R. Feagin, "Black Politics in the South: A Descriptive Analysis," Unpublished Manuscript, Austin: University of Texas, March 1974.

Conyers, James E., William J. Farmer, and Martin Levin, *Black Youth in a Southern Metropolis,* Atlanta: Southern Regional Council, 1968.

Feagin, Joe R. and Harlan Hahn, "The Second Reconstruction: Black Political Strength in the South," *Social Science Quarterly,* Vol. 51, June 1970, 42–56.

Fleming, G. James, "The Negro in American Politics: The Past," in John P. Davis, editor, *The American Negro Reference Book,* Englewood Cliffs, N.J.: Prentice-Hall, 1966.

Ginzberg, Eli and Dale L. Hiestand, "Employment Patterns of Negro Men and Women," in John P. Davis, editor, *The American Negro Reference Book,* Englewood Cliffs, N.J.: Prentice-Hall, 1966.

Goodman, Leo A. and William G. Kruskal, "Measures of Association for Cross-Classification," *Journal of the American Statistical Association,* 1954, Vol. 69, 732–764.

Harris, Louis, a poll reported in *Time* magazine, April 6, 1970.

Hatcher, Richard G., "The Black Role in Urban Politics," *Current History,* November 1969, 287–293.

Hovland, C. I., A. Lumsdaine, and F. D. Sheffield, *Experiments in Mass Communication,* Princeton, N.J.: Princeton University Press, 1949.

Johnson, Tobe, *Metropolitan Government: A Black Analytical Perspective,* Washington, D.C.: Joint Center for Political Studies, 1972.

Joint Center for Political Studies, *National Roster of Black Elected Officials,* Vols. 1–4, Washington, D.C., March 1971, March 1972, May 1973, and April 1974.

Jones, Mack, "Black Officeholders in Local Governments of the South: An Overview," in *Politics '71: Problems of Political Participation,* Greenville, N.C.: East Carolina University Press, 1971.

Kerlinger, F., "Social Attitude Scales," in M. Shaw and J. Wright, *Scales for the Measurement of Attitudes,* New York: McGraw-Hill, 1967.

Kilson, Martin, "Black Politics: A New Power," *Dissent,* August 1971, 333–345.

Lane, Robert E., *Political Life: Why People Get Involved in Politics*, Glencoe, Ill.: Free Press, 1959.

Matthews, Donald R. and James W. Prothro, "Social and Economic Factors and Negro Voter Registration in the South," *American Political Science Review*, Vol. LVII, no. 1 (March 1963), 24–44.

Metropolitan Applied Research Center and Voter Education Project, *National Roster of Black Elected Officials*, Washington, D.C., February 1970.

Merton, Robert K., "Patterns of Influence: Local and Cosmopolitan Influentials," in Robert K. Merton, *Social Theory and Social Structure*, revised and enlarged, Glencoe, Ill.: Free Press, 1957.

Miller, Arthur, Thad Brown, and Alden Raine, "Social Conflict and Political Estrangement, 1958–1972," paper read at 1973 meeting of Midwest Political Science Association.

Pinkney, Alphonso, *Black Americans*, Englewood Cliffs, N.J.: Prentice-Hall, 1969.

Robinson, John P., Jerrold G. Rusk, and Kendra B. Head, *Measures of Political Attitudes*, Ann Arbor, Mich.: Institute for Social Research, 1968.

Selznick, Gertrude and Stephen Steinberg, "Class and Ideology in the 1964 Election: A National Survey," paper presented at the August 1966 meeting of the American Sociological Association.

Sloan, Lee and Robert M. French, "Black Rule in the Urban South," *Trans-Action*, November-December 1971, 29–33.

U.S. Department of Commerce, Bureau of the Census, *Historical Statistics of the United States: Colonial Times to 1957*, Washington, D.C.: U.S. Government Printing Office, 1960.

——, *Statistical Abstract of the United States*, Washington, D.C.: U.S. Government Printing Office, 1973.

Walton, Hanes, Jr., *Black Politics: A Theoretical and Structural Analysis*, Philadelphia, Pa.: J. B. Lippincott, 1972.

Wilson, James Q., "The Negro in Politics," *Daedalus*, Vol. 94, no. 4, Fall 1965.

——, "The Negro in American Politics: The Present," in John P. Davis, editor, *The American Negro Reference Book*, Englewood Cliffs, N.J.: Prentice-Hall, 1966.

Woodward, C. Vann, *The Strange Career of Jim Crow*, 2nd rev. ed., New York: Oxford University Press, 1966.

Appendix A

A NATIONAL SURVEY OF BLACK
ELECTED OFFICIALS IN THE UNITED STATES

Under the sponsorship of Russell Sage Foundation, I am conducting a national study of black elected officials, of whom you are one. This unprecedented study should provide a clear social description of this new and vitally important group of officeholders.

The following questionnaire inquires about certain aspects of your background as well as your political relations, expectations, and attitudes toward contemporary political and social issues. The questionnaire should, if possible, be completed *rapidly and in one sitting*. It should not take more than *30 minutes* to complete.

Some of the information requested is of a personal nature but *the information you give will not be connected with your name. Please do not write your name on the questionnaire or on the return envelope.* However, please sign and return the enclosed self-addressed postcard independently of your completed questionnaire. This postcard will be our only way of knowing whether you have returned the questionnaire. There will be no way of matching returned questionnaires with returned postcards.

Thank you for your kind cooperation and assistance, and if you have any questions about the study, please contact me at the following address:

Professor James E. Conyers
Department of Sociology
Indiana State University
Terre Haute, Indiana 47809

Questionnaire

Political Background

1. What is your present party affiliation?
   - _____ Democrat
   - _____ Republican
   - _____ Independent
   - _____ Other _____
     (specify)
2. Have you ever changed your political party affiliation?
   a. _____yes, when I was _____ years old.
   b. _____ no
   c. if yes, *from* what party *to* what party?

   _____
   (specify)
3. To which of the following types of office were you *most recently* elected? (Check *one*.)
   - _____ U.S. Senator or Congressman
   - _____ State Senator or Representative
   - _____ Other State Office _____
     (specify)
   - _____ County Commissioner, Supervisor or Election Commissioner
   - _____ Other County Office _____
     (specify)
   - _____ City Mayor or Vice Mayor
   - _____ Councilman or Alderman
   - _____ Other City Office _____
     (specify)
   - _____ Judge or Magistrate
   - _____ Constable or Marshal
   - _____ Justice of the Peace or other Law Enforcement Office _____
     (specify)
   - _____ School Board Member
   - _____ Other Education Office

   _____
   (specify)

4. To which other types of office have you ever been elected? (Check as many as apply.)
   - _____ U.S. Senator or Congressman
   - _____ State Senator or Representative
   - _____ Other State Office _____
     (specify)
   - _____ County Commissioner, Supervisor or Election Commissioner
   - _____ Other County Office _____
     (specify)
   - _____ City Mayor or Vice Mayor
   - _____ Councilman or Alderman
   - _____ Other City Office _____
     (specify)
   - _____ Judge or Magistrate
   - _____ Constable or Marshal
   - _____ Justice of the Peace or other Law Enforcement Office _____
     (specify)
   - _____ School Board Member
   - _____ Other Education Office

   _____
   (specify)
5. Approximate number of people in the area or district from which you were elected, including those not of voting age.

   _____ (number)
6. Roughly what per cent of the people in the area or district from which you were most recently elected is Black, including those not of voting age?

   _____ (per cent)
7. On what date did you formally take your present office?

   _____ (date)

NOTE: Black officials and White officials were asked the same questions, except question 49, which was asked of Black officials only.

8. From which of the following regions of the country were you elected to public office most recently? (Check *one*.)
   _____ South Atlantic (includes Md., Del., W.Va., N.C., S.C., Ga., Fla., Va. and Washington, D.C.)
   _____ East South Central (includes Ky., Tenn., Ala. and Miss.)
   _____ West South Central (includes Okla., Ark., Texas and La.)
   _____ Middle Atlantic (includes N.Y., N.J. and Pa.)
   _____ New England (includes Conn., Mass., N.H., Vt., R.I. and Me.)
   _____ East North Central (includes Wis., Ill., Ind., Mich. and Ohio)
   _____ West North Central (includes Minn., Iowa, Mo., Kans., Nebr., S. Dak. and N. Dak.)
   _____ Mountain West (includes N. Mex., Ariz., Nev., Utah, Colo., Wyo., Idaho and Mont.)
   _____ Pacific West (includes Calif., Oregon and Wash.)
   _____ Non-continental U.S.A. (includes Alaska, Puerto Rico and Hawaii)

9. How many different times have you run for public office?
   a. in primary elections _____
      (number)
   b. in general elections _____
      (number)

10. Did you have an opponent running against you:
   a. in your most recent primary election campaign?
      _____ yes _____ no
   b. in your most recent general election campaign?
      _____ yes _____ no

11. How old were you when you were *first* elected to public office?
   _____

12. How many different times have you been elected to public office?
   _____
   (number)

13. How many years in all have you served as an elected government official of any kind?
   _____
   (number of years)

14. How long have you lived in the community from which you were elected to your present office?
   _____

15. What is the annual salary of the public office you now hold?
   $_____

16. What were your gross annual earnings from all sources between January 1, 1970 and January 1, 1971? (include your salary from elected office)
   _____ under $10,000
   _____ $10,000 to $19,999
   _____ $20,000 to $29,999
   _____ $30,000 to $39,999
   _____ $40,000 to $49,999
   _____ over $50,000

Educational Background

17. Did you attend or complete high school?
   _____ yes, and graduated
   _____ no, I never attended
   _____ yes, but did not graduate

18. Are you presently enrolled in any educational institution part-time or full-time?
   _____ yes _____ no

19. If you attended or completed high school, was the high school:
   _____ almost all Black _____ about ¼ Black
   _____ about ¾ Black _____ almost all White
   _____ about ½ Black

20. If you attended or completed high school, was the high school:
    a. publicly supported? _____   b. privately supported? _____
21. Please list in the table below any college, university or other higher education you have received.

Name of Institution	Location (City & State)	Years Attended From	To	Major Field Name	Minor Field Name	Degree (if any) Type	Year Granted

22. If you have received any honorary degrees, please list them.

Type of Honorary Degree	Year Received	Institution Conferring Degree

23. Education of parents:
    a. Father's highest grade or degree completed _____
    b. Mother's highest grade or degree completed _____

Work Background

24. What was your *first* full-time job after you got out of school?

25. What different jobs did you hold before you were elected to public office?

26. What was your *last* occupation before you became an elected official?

27. At present, do you actively work in some other occupation in addition to your job as an elected official?
    a. yes _____   b. no _____
    c. If yes, what is it?

28. Principal occupation of parents (if either or both parents are now dead or retired, indicate occupation prior to death or retirement):
    a. Father's principal occupation:
    _____
    b. Mother's principal occupation:
    _____

Personal and Family Background

29. Sex: Male _____   Female _____
30. Year of birth: _____

31. In which of the following regions did you mainly grow up? (Check *one*.)
    _____ South Atlantic (includes Md., Del., W.Va., N.C., S.C., Ga., Fla., Va. and Washington, D.C.)
    _____ East South Central (includes Ky., Tenn., Ala. and Miss.)
    _____ West South Central (includes Okla., Ark., Texas and La.)
    _____ Middle Atlantic (includes N.Y., N.J. and Pa.)
    _____ New England (includes Conn., Mass., N.H., Vt., R.I. and Me.)
    _____ East North Central (includes Wis., Ill., Ind., Mich. and Ohio)
    _____ West North Central (includes Minn., Iowa, Mo., Kans., Nebr., S. Dak. and N. Dak.)
    _____ Mountain West (includes N. Mex., Ariz., Nev., Utah, Colo., Wyo., Idaho and Mont.)
    _____ Pacific West (includes Calif., Oregon and Wash.)
    _____ Non-continental U.S.A. (includes Alaska, Puerto Rico and Hawaii)
    _____ Other _____
    (specify)

32. How large was the community in which you mainly grew up? (Check *one*.)
    _____ under 2,500
    _____ 2,500 to 10,000
    _____ 10,000 to 25,000
    _____ 25,000 to 100,000
    _____ 100,000 to 500,000
    _____ over 500,000

33. Present marital status:
    _____ currently married
    _____ never married
    _____ currently widowed, not married
    _____ currently separated or divorced

34. How many children do you have?
    _____
    (number)

35. How many brothers and sisters were there in your family when you were growing up? (Do not count yourself.) _____
    (number)

36. If you have had brothers and sisters, how many were born and lived through infancy before you were? _____
    (number)

37. What is your present religious affiliation, if any? _____
    (specify)

38. How often do you attend church?
    _____ about once a week or more
    _____ about two or three times a month
    _____ about once a month
    _____ about three or four times a year
    _____ about once a year
    _____ almost never or never

39. Would you say that you are: _____ very religious _____ somewhat religious _____ not very religious _____ not religious at all

40. Do you hold membership in any of the following types of organizations or groups?

Type Of Organization	Membership		Hold Office		How Many Specific Organizations Of This Type Do You Belong To?
	Yes	No	Yes	No	
Patriotic, military & veterans					
Civic and service					
Fraternal and lodges					
Economic, occupational, professional					
Religious or church affiliated					
Political and social reform					
Social and recreational					
Cultural, educational, alumni					

Political Relations

41. Here are some individuals and groups who may have been helpful or detrimental *to your most recent election*. Please place an "X" in the appropriate box for each.

Individuals And Groups	Mainly Helped My Election		Neither Helped Nor Hindered My Election	Mainly Hindered My Election
	Very Much	Somewhat		
Family and close personal friends				
Party leaders				
Black organizations and leaders not in government				
Black leaders in government				
The unorganized Black population				
Predominantly White organizations and leaders not in government				
White leaders in government				
The unorganized White population				
Mass media (newspapers, radio, TV)				
Campaign workers				

Other (specify)

_____

_____

42. Here are some individuals and groups who may be helpful or detrimental *to your performance of duties in your present office*. Please place an "X" in the appropriate box for each.

Individuals And Groups	Mainly Help My Performance of Duties		Neither Help Nor Hinder My Performance of Duties	Mainly Hinder My Performance of Duties
	Very Much	Some-what		
Family and close personal friends				
Party leaders				
Black organizations and leaders not in government				
Black leaders in government				
The unorganized Black population				
Predominantly White organizations and leaders not in government				
White leaders in government				
The unorganized White population				
Mass media (newspapers, radio, TV)				
Campaign workers				
Other (specify)				

43. How often do the following individuals and groups *contact* you for the purpose of getting your support or getting you to act in some way in your role as a public official?

Individuals And Groups	Contact Me Very Often	Contact Me Sometimes	Contact Me Rarely	Contact Me Never
Family and close personal friends				
Party leaders				

Black organizations and leaders   not in government

Black leaders in government

The unorganized Black population

Predominantly White organizations   and leaders not in government

White leaders in government

The unorganized White population

Mass media (newspapers,   radio, TV)

Campaign workers

Other (specify)

44. On the whole, do you think you have made *mostly friends or mostly enemies* among the following individuals and groups as a result of being an elected official? Please place an "X" in the appropriate boxes.

Individuals And Groups	Made Mostly Friends	Made Mostly Enemies	Made Both Friends and Enemies	Made Neither Friends Nor Enemies
Family and close personal friends				
Party leaders				
Black organizations and leaders not in government				
Black leaders in government				
The unorganized Black population				
Predominantly White organizations and leaders not in government				
White leaders in government				
The unorganized White population				
Mass media (newspapers, radio, TV)				
Campaign workers				
Other (specify)				

45. In what ways did your race make a difference, for better or worse, in *getting elected* to your present office?

_____
_____
_____
_____

46. In what ways does your race make a difference, for better or worse, *in your performance of duties* in your present office?

_____
_____
_____
_____

47. How important to you personally are the following possible reasons for seeking public office? Please rank them from 1 to 4, counting 1 as "most important" and 4 as "least important."

_____ a desire to correct social injustices

_____ a desire to have the public prestige and personal income that goes with government office

_____ a desire to be "on the inside" and "near the center of things"

_____ a desire to serve my country

48. Do you expect to (please check *one*):

_____ run again for your present office

_____ run for some higher public office

_____ run for some other, not necessarily higher, public office

_____ retire from public life after your present term

_____ Other (specify):
_____

49. In your opinion, how important are each of the following in achieving real progress for Blacks in America?

	Very Important	Fairly Important	Not Too Important	Not Important At All
a. More Black political control of Black communities	_____	_____	_____	_____
b. More Black-owned businesses	_____	_____	_____	_____
c. More Black studies programs in high schools and colleges	_____	_____	_____	_____
d. More Black-controlled schools and universities	_____	_____	_____	_____
e. Complete racial integration in schools and universities	_____	_____	_____	_____

f. More Black partners, direc-
    tors, managers, etc., of
    predominantly White
    businesses   _____ _____ _____ _____
g. Formation of an indepen-
    dent all-Black political
    party   _____ _____ _____ _____
h. Formation of an indepen-
    dent, but not all-Black,
    all-minority political party _____ _____ _____ _____
i. Working through the
    established party structure _____ _____ _____ _____
j. More Black elected officials
    in the established govern-
    mental system   _____ _____ _____ _____
k. Complete racial integration
    within this nation   _____ _____ _____ _____
l. Complete racial segrega-
    tion within this nation _____ _____ _____ _____
m. Mass public demonstra-
    tions, sit-ins, marches, etc. _____ _____ _____ _____
n. The use of violence when
    peaceful methods fail _____ _____ _____ _____
o. Non-violence   _____ _____ _____ _____
p. Court actions and
    legislation   _____ _____ _____ _____
q. Petitions and delegations
r. Greater control of hard
    drugs   _____ _____ _____ _____
s. Free health and day-care
    centers   _____ _____ _____ _____
t. Birth-control   _____ _____ _____ _____
u. Stopping the war in
    Vietnam   _____ _____ _____ _____
v. Water and air pollution
    programs   _____ _____ _____ _____
w. More emphasis on law
    and order   _____ _____ _____ _____
x. A national cut-back on
    missile building and outer
    space programs   _____ _____ _____ _____

Attitudes Toward Political and Social Issues

50. Below is a list of statements dealing with contemporary values and issues. Please check whether you *strongly agree, agree, disagree, strongly disagree,* or have *no opinion* about each statement.

	Strongly Agree	Agree	No Opinion	Disagree	Strongly Disagree
1. In recent times this country hase moved dangerously close to socialism.	____	____	____	____	____
2. In recent times this country has moved dangerously close to fascism.	____	____	____	____	____
3. All groups can live in harmony in this country without changing the system in any way.	____	____	____	____	____
4. If you start trying to change things very much, you usually make them worse.	____	____	____	____	____
5. A first consideration in any society is the protection of property rights.	____	____	____	____	____
6. Inherited racial characteristics play more of a part in the achievement of individuals and groups than is generally thought.	____	____	____	____	____
7. True democracy is limited in the United States because of the special privileges enjoyed by business and industry.	____	____	____	____	____
8. There are too many professors in our colleges and universities who are radical in their social and political beliefs.	____	____	____	____	____
9. It is the responsibility of the entire society, through its government, to guarantee everyone adequate housing, income and leisure.	____	____	____	____	____

10. Americans may not be
    perfect, but the American
    Way has brought us
    about as close as human
    beings can get to a
    perfect society. ·   _____ _____ _____ _____ _____
11. Marriages between White
    and Black people should
    be discouraged.   _____ _____ _____ _____ _____
12. Sometimes you have to
    cheat a little to get what
    you want.   _____ _____ _____ _____ _____
13. When you get right down
    to it, most policemen are
    pretty good guys.   _____ _____ _____ _____ _____
14. When people talk about
    birth control, they really
    mean birth control for
    Black people, not White
    people.   _____ _____ _____ _____ _____
15. Marijuana should be
    legalized.   _____ _____ _____ _____ _____
16. Women should have the
    same social, economic,
    and political rights as men,
    even if it involves taking
    some rights away from
    men.   _____ _____ _____ _____ _____
17. Student unrest is largely
    caused by a lack of
    parental guidance.   _____ _____ _____ _____ _____
18. Student unrest on most
    college campuses is part
    of a larger conspiracy to
    undermine the forces of
    law and order in
    American society.   _____ _____ _____ _____ _____

PLEASE READ!

Now that you have completed the questionnaire, please check to see if you have signed and returned the enclosed self-addressed postcard independently of your completed questionnaire. The questionnaire itself is to be placed separately in the self-addressed envelope and mailed to me. Let me thank you again for your kind cooperation and assistance.

If you have additional comments you would like to make about the study, please feel free to do so in the space provided below.

Appendix B

I. a. What elected office do you hold at present? _____

  b. In what state? _____

  c. In what county or city? _____

II. In general, what difference do you feel your election to office has made? To the Black community? (probe)

To the White community? (probe)

III. What has been the *biggest problem or obstacle* you have had in the performance of your duties as an elected official?
In the Black community? (probe)

In the White community? (probe)

IV. As an elected official, what has been your *biggest aid or help* in the performance of duties associated with the office you hold?
In the Black community? (probe)

In the White community? (probe)

V. What do you see as your *greatest need* as an elected official?

VI. In your opinion, what is the future of race relations in America?

VII. In your opinion, what is the future of this country?
In domestic affairs? (probe)

In international affairs? (probe)

VIII. Finally, in your opinion, what is the future of Black elected officials?
In your particular locality? (probe)

In the United States generally? (probe)

Appendix C

CUTTING-POINTS (MEDIANS) FOR STANDARDIZATION[a] OF POPULATION SIZE AND PERCENT BLACK BY TYPE OF OFFICE

Type of Office	Black Officials Population Size	Percent Black	White Officials Population Size	Percent Black
State	> 100,000	> 60	> 750,000	> 7
County	> 25,000	> 60	> 25,000	> 35
City	> 25,000	> 45	> 25,000	> 18
Law	> 500,000	> 30	> 200,000	> 37
Education	> 50,000	> 28	> 25,000	> 1

[a]All election areas that were above the indicated medians for the types of offices held by respondents were classified as "High"; all those at or below medians were classified as "Low." For example, Black state level officials coming from election areas having populations of more than 100,000 and Black city level officials coming from election areas having populations of more than 25,000 were classified together as "High" in population size. Similarly, Black state officials coming from election areas whose populations were more than 60 percent Black and Black education officials coming from areas whose populations were more than 28 percent Black were classified together as "High" in percent Black.

Appendix D

SELECTED CHARACTERISTICS (PERCENT, UNLESS OTHERWISE
INDICATED) NOT INCLUDED IN THE ANALYSIS

	Black Sample	White Sample
Father's Occupation:		
Professional, technical, and kindred	18	18
Managers, administrators (except farm)	8	25
Sales, clerical, crafts, and kindred	18	28
Operators, laborers (except farm), service	34	9
Farmers, farm laborers, managers, and foremen	18	17
Housewives, retired, unemployed	3	2
Total	99[a] (683)[b]	99[a] (422)[b]
Father's Education High School or More	37 (688)	54 (446)
Mother's Education High School or More	43 (715)	56 (440)
Median Number of Brothers and Sisters	3.4 (792)	2.4 (484)
Married	88	94
Never Married	3	3
Widowed	4	2
Separated or Divorced	5	2
Total	100 (793)	101 (483)
Median Number of Children	2.3 (788)	2.7 (479)
Consider Self Very Religious	31 (775)	24 (475)
Religious Affiliation:		
Baptist	38	18
Protestant (unspecified)	15	9
Methodist (unspecified)	14	16
Catholic	9	28

[a] Total percentages may not sum to 100 because of rounding error.

[b] Total N's may not sum to the full sample sizes (Black = 799; White = 486) because of No Answers and Don't Knows.

	Black Sample	White Sample
Episcopalian	6	6
Presbyterian	5	6
Other	13	17
Total	100 (747)	100 (451)
Church Attendance:		
About once a week	44	56
Two or three times a month	21	11
Once a month to once a year	31	26
Almost never or never	5	7
Total	101 (789)	100 (475)
High School Education or More	90 (793)	92 (481)
College Education or More	77 (610)	78 (351)
Now Enrolled in Educational Institution	13 (771)	4 (468)
Median Number of Months in Current Office	32 (716)	34 (420)
Median Age at First Election	42 (777)	39 (476)
Median Number of Years in All Elected Offices	3.5 (729)	6.0 (466)
Political Expectations:		
Run again for present office	55	46
Run for higher office	18	11
Run for other (not nec. higher) office	4	6
Retire from public life after current office	12	31
Other	11	6
Total	100 (714)	100 (449)
Median Salary From Current Office	$1,200 (751)	$987 (456)
Median Gross Income in 1970	$15,265 (747)	$18,785 (454)
Present Employment Outside Current Elected Office:		
Professional, technical, and kindred	44	28
Managers, administrators (except farm)	21	27
Sales, clerical, crafts, and kindred	14	12
Operators, laborers (except farm), service	5	1
Farmers, farm laborers, managers, and foremen	2	6
Housewives, retired, unemployed	14	25
Total	100 (658)	99 (444)

	Black Sample	White Sample
"Agreeing:"		
When you get right down to it, most policemen are pretty good guys.	59 (771)	91 (474)
Americans may not be perfect, but the American Way has brought us about as close as human beings can get to a perfect society.	44 (761)	74 (471)
Student unrest is largely caused by a lack of parental guidance.	37 (767)	55 (470)
All groups can live in harmony in this country without changing the system in any way.	22 (778)	41 (469)
Marijuana should be legalized.	16 (769)	8 (472)
If you start trying to change things very much, you usually make them worse.	11 (768)	22 (472)
Marriages between White and Black people should be discouraged.	6 (776)	53 (465)
"Very Important" for "Real Progress for Blacks in America[c]:"		
More Black elected officials in government	95 (780)	
Greater control of hard drugs	88 (767)	
Stopping the war in Vietnam	84 (770)	
More Black political control of Black communities	78 (763)	
Complete racial integration within this nation	76 (773)	
Water and air pollution programs	65 (755)	
Non-violence	64 (738)	
Cutback on missile building and outer space programs	54 (759)	
More Black studies programs in high schools and colleges	48 (772)	
More emphasis on law and order	41 (743)	
Independent but not all-Black minority political party	20 (729)	
Complete racial segregation within this nation	4 (676)	

---

[c] Question asked of Black sample only.

Index